The
VEGAN
LIFESTYLE
JOURNAL

**All you need to feel confident & empowered
to become an ethical vegan**

This journal belongs to

Published by Luna Wolf Books

First published in Great Britain in 2022

ISBN 978-1-3999-1520-5

Printed and bound in Great Britain by TJ Books

Cover art by BookSmith Design

Interior design by Softwood Self-Publishing

CONTENTS

Welcome to the Vegan Lifestyle Journal.

I'm so excited you're here. For whatever reason you picked up this book, be it intrigue about veganism, wondering how you can adopt the beliefs into your own life, or wanting to take your veganism a step further, this journal has totally got your back!

Going vegan can seem daunting at first. But have no fear! The chapters inside are designed perfectly to break it all down into manageable chunks and guide you to focus on what's important to you and how to make those changes. This is everything I wish I'd had when I first went vegan. It's easy to follow, fun to fill out, and is suitable for people at all stages of their journey. You can work through it start to finish or navigate to the sections that are most important to you. Make use of the blank pages at the back to keep all your notes organised in one place as you go.

Ethical veganism, at its core, is about ending the suffering and exploitation of animals through any means. It is a set of beliefs that can impact all areas of your life, including the clothing you wear, the food you eat, your social activities, entertainment you attend, where you travel, how you raise your children, and more. Although vegans share the same beliefs, there can be variances in practice, and it all comes down to you as a person, what your morals and motivations are, and how you feel about certain things. We'll cover these scenarios as they come up in each chapter.

When you start to think about the ways in which animals are exploited for and by humans, it spans into many different areas, so chapters have been designed to help you make sense of them all and take control of what you want to change in your life. Some of the topics we're going to cover can be heavy (cue animal rights and climate change), but ultimately, this is an exploration of values and beliefs and will fundamentally change your life for the better!

Each of us has the ability to affect huge change in the world and end animal suffering. This journal is going to empower you to do exactly that!

Sadie
XO

CHAPTER ONE

INTRODUCTION

Veganism is a philosophy and way of living which seeks to exclude, as far as is possible and practicable, all forms of exploitation of and cruelty to animals for food, clothing, or any other purpose.

The Vegan Society

Why go vegan?

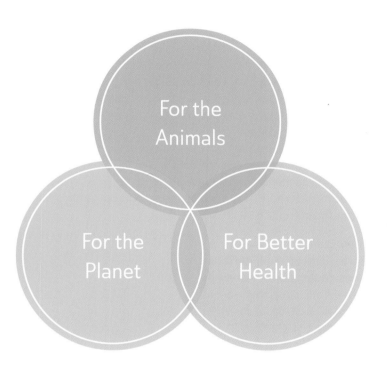

For the
Animals

For the
Planet

For Better
Health

For the Animals

Animals are currently exploited in a multitude of ways; the top reasons being for food, entertainment, clothing, and science. Caring about animals and wanting to end their suffering is at the heart of ethical veganism.

Food

It goes without saying that taking meat off your plate will dramatically help reduce animal suffering. Every year, 72 billion land animals and over 1.2 trillion aquatic animals are killed for food around the world. That's around 3 billion per day![1]

Many of the animals farmed for food are reared in intensive factory farming environments and are killed at just a fraction of their normal life span. Selective breeding has made some animals so different to their natural state that they experience multiple health issues, such as hens, who are bred to grow so large, so fast, that they struggle to move or even stand up, leaving them to spend most of their short lives lying in their own waste, with open sores and wounds that act as gateways to infection.[2] Even if animals are reared free-range, they all ultimately end up on a slaughterhouse kill floor. There is no happy ending for an animal bred for food.

Methods of killing animals varies depending on the country, but the term 'humane slaughter' is a clever marketing gimmick created to make us feel better about the way animals die for food. Ultimately, there is no humane way to kill an animal that doesn't want to die. Take pigs for example; more intelligent than dogs, it is reported that the 'best practice model' for their slaughter in the UK leaves them 'kicking out and screaming' before death, just after they are forced into gas chambers and killed.[3] A personal account from a slaughterhouse worker recalls how the "cows being brought in would get scared and panic".[4]

However, animals don't just suffer for meat production; they are also exploited for other resources they produce, like milk from cows and eggs from hens. Animals exploited for these types of products can live in some appalling conditions, seen only as profit commodities. They are then killed at a significantly younger age than natural when their bodies are spent and no longer useful to the industry.

There is a gross amount of waste in these industries. Male calves are mostly shot at just one day old because their mother's milk is being sold to humans, and if they aren't killed immediately, they are sold for veal: another cruel industry. Baby male chicks are seen as a waste product of the egg industry because they offer no financial gain as they don't lay eggs, so are usually gassed or killed via maceration (ground alive) at just one day old.

Animal farming has become unsustainable and unbelievably inhumane. Animals are sentient beings[5] that have the ability to feel pain and emotions. In the same way our dog would yelp if we stood on its foot, cows, pigs, and other farmed animals yelp or wail when they experience pain. Mother cows display grief emotions by crying out for days when their calves are taken from them so that humans can drink the mother's milk. It is unnecessary to exploit them and make them suffer for our food when we can lead healthy and happy lives on a vegan diet.[6]

Entertainment
Another reason for wanting to become an ethical vegan is to help stop abuse or neglect of animals that are exploited for human entertainment, such as in zoos, aquariums, or for horse/dog racing. These animals can suffer in many ways, from being taken from their families and natural habitats in the wild to being forced to perform in environments they aren't used to. Many animals in captivity lead sad and lonely existences and have much shorter lifespans.

Clothing
Animals farmed for fashion live miserable lives, often in cramped conditions, and face unthinkable suffering when they are killed for their pelts. We usually just think of cows being killed for their skin (leather) as a waste product of the meat industry, but the leather industry is much bigger in comparison. Dogs are also killed for their skin and can be sold as 'leather', so you might not actually be buying cow hide! In some of the countries that are the biggest producers of leather, cows and dogs have been filmed being skinned alive, which is not uncommon practice. For more on animals used in fashion, see the 'Lifestyle' chapter.

Science
Vivisection, the practice of performing operations on live animals for the purpose of experimentation or scientific research, is another prominent animal rights issue. Animals are used to test the safety of cosmetics, pesticides, drugs, chemicals, and other products, as well as for researching disease cures and prevention. For more on animals used in science, see the 'Personal Care' chapter.

Although ethical veganism is centred around ending animal suffering, there are some other important factors that motivate people to eat a vegan diet or lead a vegan lifestyle, the main two being health and environment.

For Better Health

Reducing and eliminating animal products from our diets and eating lots of fresh fruits, vegetables, nuts, legumes, and grains can have massive health benefits, both physically and emotionally, which is why it is a popular reason for some people to turn to veganism. Often those who start out with this motivation of better health carry on down the path of a full vegan lifestyle.

Physical benefits
Following a well-balanced, vegan diet has been shown to reduce the risk of certain diseases. A study conducted by the National Cancer Centre found that people who follow a vegan diet are at the lowest risk of cancer, heart disease, and hypertension, compared with other diets.[7]

Dr Campbell, author of The China Study, says that in multiple, peer-reviewed animal studies, researchers discovered that they could actually turn the growth of cancer cells on and off by raising and lowering doses of casein (on by raising the dose, off by lowering the dose), the main protein found in cow's milk.[8] Findings in The China Study also show that people who ate the most animal-based foods got the most chronic disease and people who ate the most plant-based foods were the healthiest.

It's also possible to reverse and prevent other conditions, such as diabetes, obesity, autoimmune diseases, bone, kidney, eye, and brain diseases. Research carried out by the British Heart Foundation shows that early deaths from heart disease, strokes, type-2 diabetes, and cancer were lower in those who ate a plant-based diet, and overall, it recommends that, "if you eat a lot of red and processed meat, cutting down and including more plant-based foods in your diet could be beneficial to both your health and the environment".[9]

Emotional benefits
The mind and body are intrinsically connected. When you improve your physical health, you naturally experience greater mental and emotional well-being.

Plant-based foods have high nutrient properties that have been linked to decreased stress levels. Foods typical to a vegan diet, such as leafy greens, fermented foods, and even dark chocolate, have been found to lower levels of cortisol, the stress hormone, in the blood. This helps to combat the stresses of our daily lives, which can ultimately reduce depression and anxiety. Vegan diets typically consist of complex carbohydrates that increase serotonin levels, also known as the feel-good hormone. All the while, meat and animal products contain long-chain fatty acids, which are linked to symptoms of depression. Incorporating more plant-based foods into your diet can positively impact your physical and mental wellbeing.[10]

Vegans often report improved emotional health benefits when transitioning to this lifestyle because they feel like they are living a life in alignment with their values. It can also be seen as a form of mindfulness when increasing awareness of what goes into your body. Some even believe that meat carries energetics of the animal, and the stress and fear it felt at slaughter (which will have triggered a physical response of hormones in the animal) is then consumed by the person eating it.

Pandemics

Covid-19 has got experts thinking urgently about the risk of diseases passing from farmed animals to humans. The vast majority of animals involved in historic zoonotic events or current zoonosis are either livestock, domesticated wildlife, or pets.[11] Some of the most commonly known outbreaks linked to animal farming over the past two centuries are bovine tuberculosis, bovine spongiform encephalopathy (BSE), bird flu, severe acute respiratory syndrome (SARS), swine flu, and Middle East respiratory syndrome (MERS).

As a result of these outbreaks, millions of people and animals have died. Animals are culled to try and prevent further spread of the outbreaks, and the methods used are horrific, such as pigs being dumped in to large, dug out pits while still alive.

Scientists are warning that our current farming methods and our demand for regular supplies of affordable meat will "create future pandemics that will make the Covid-19 pandemic look like a dress rehearsal".[12] There really is no time like the present to re-think our approach to eating animals for the sake of our health.

For the Planet

The last of the motivations for becoming a vegan, but by no means the least, is the planet. Some people chose to go vegan because of their desire to protect the environment and reduce their carbon footprint.

Emissions

The most thorough and comprehensive assessment of food production on the global environment to date advises that huge reductions in meat-eating are essential to avoid dangerous climate change.[13] The UN states that livestock farming is responsible for 14.5% of global greenhouse gas emissions,[14] with the majority of that coming from beef and cattle milk production, closely followed by pig meat, poultry, and eggs. That puts animal agriculture emissions on par with emissions from all the planes, trains, automobiles, and ships around the world.[15] Researchers at the University of Oxford found that cutting meat and dairy products from your diet could reduce an individual's carbon footprint by a massive 73%, and stated that eating a vegan diet could be the "single biggest way" to reduce your environmental impact on earth.[16]

Habitat loss

In 2020, 42,000 square km of tropical rainforest were lost—that's an area twice the size of the country of Wales, or equivalent of nine football fields disappearing every minute of every day, all just to make way for animal agriculture.[17] Extensive cattle ranching is the number one culprit of deforestation in virtually every Amazon country, and accounts for 80% of current deforestation.[18]

Both in the Amazon, but also anywhere else globally, land that is allocated solely to raising animals for food leads to huge biodiversity and habitat loss, with much of the world having lost a large amount of its natural biodiversity already. According to a study by Oxford University, biodiversity is the most complex feature of our planet, and it is the most vital. Without it, "there is no future for humanity".[19]

But there is a way forward. If everyone shifted to a plant-based diet, we would reduce global land use for agriculture by 75%.[20] That's the majority of all the world's cropland! This would be possible thanks to a reduction in land used for grazing and a smaller need for land to grow crops. We are growing a phenomenal number of crops just to feed animals and then kill them. It's hugely inefficient. Take a look at the comparison chart below on the land required to feed 1 person for 1 year, broken down by diet:[21]

› **Vegan:** 1/6th acre

› **Vegetarian:** 3x as much as a vegan

› **Meat Eater:** 18x as much as a vegan

Waste

Another dirty industry secret is the waste from farms. All that poop has to go somewhere, and there are many environmental studies, reports, and even fines from environmental agencies, where farm waste run-off has been disposed of incorrectly and ended up in waterways. This waste contains high levels of nitrogen and phosphorus, so when it flows into lakes, rivers, or oceans, it acts like a fertilizer. This fertilizer causes algae bloom that, when it dies off, starves the water of oxygen, creating huge dead zones where no sea life can live.[22]

There are a ton of wasted resources when it comes to farming animals too. It takes 167 liters of water to produce one vegan burger but 1,000 liters of water to produce one beef burger—that's six times the quantity of water to make the meat version. Skipping one hamburger per week for a year saves 22,100 gallons of water, which is equivalent to flushing your toilet nearly 38 times a day for a year.[23]

The fishing industry is having devastating effects on the oceans with the waste it produces. Approximately 46% of the 79,000 tons of plastic in the Great Pacific Garbage Patch is made up of fishing nets, ropes, FADs (fish aggregating devices), long lines, and plastic fishing crates and baskets that have either been purposefully or accidentally lost, discarded, or abandoned.[24] This discarded fishing gear will continue to devastate natural habitats for decades by entangling or suffocating fish, sharks, whales, dolphins, sea turtles, seals, and marine birds. Plastic in the ocean will never disappear; it will continue to break down until it becomes microscopic and is ingested by countless marine animals. This is already happening and, shockingly, studies are showing that the fish that humans are eating have already ingested microplastics.[25]

Corporate responsibilities

Whilst it's important for us to make individual change, it's also worth noting the large-scale impact some companies have on the environment. Just 100 companies have been the source of more than 70% of the world's greenhouse gas emissions since 1988, according to The Carbon Majors Report.[26] Aside from emissions, let's also think about waste. It's all well and good putting the onus on the consumer to recycle, but how about holding to account the organisations that aren't changing their production methods to more sustainable solutions? Start with the creator of the issue, rather than the consumer who ends up being part of it. Multinational brands are contributing to plastic pollution across the globe and these corporations, in fact all manufacturers of products, should be accountable for the waste they are generating in producing their goods. Consumer responsibilities are just a fraction of the bigger picture.

A viable human future requires a radical rethinking of our relationship to animals and the earth.

Dr Steve Best

Why I went vegan

I have loved animals my whole life. I was devoted to my cat, Jasmine, who I loved for 17 years growing up. I've always been the person rescuing sick or injured animals, stopping at the side of the road for a pheasant that's been clipped by a car to take it to the nearest vets. I was even half a day late for work once trying to get a baby bird back into the nest of a tree it had fell out of. I have volunteered at rescue centres and fostered around 50 animals in my own home. My friend Amy describes me like snow white when she sings out and all the animals come. This is how she and others close to me view me. At one with animals and nature.

There are two clear memories I have that stand out, when the reality of animal suffering started to prick through to my conscious mind.

The first memory is from when I was about 10 years old. Walking through the town centre with my mum, I saw a table with huge pictures draped over the front of it showing animals in laboratories. It was run by a group of activists campaigning to end experimentation on animals for science and cosmetics. I was horrified that anyone could do that to an animal.

The second is from when I was in my late teens, when I learned about Huntingdon Life Sciences, an evil place that carries out cruel experiments on animals and has a history of neglect and abuse, on top of the harrowing things they are already doing in the name of 'science'. This place is in my country. This is happening in my back yard. Animal experimentation was no longer a thing I considered as far away.

With those considerations swirling round in my mind about animal suffering, I got to my early 20s and it suddenly dawned on me that I couldn't love

animals and eat them as well. My whole world turned upside down. I knew I had to live my life in line with my beliefs: that animals deserve to live a life free from harm.

I suddenly realised that all animals are capable of feeling and emotions; that they are sentient beings. How had I been so brainwashed into thinking it was okay to kill some animals for food, but that you rescue and love others? There is no difference. They all have the capacity to experience suffering.

I had even gone on the whole journey of eating grass-fed, organic, and free-range meats, thinking that was the good and right thing to do. It became clear to me that was an illusion, something to make me feel better about the fact that animals were still dying for me to eat them. The animals that are grass-fed, raised organically, or even free-range, are still exploited in a number of ways and still all end up on the kill floor. How had I been so unaware?

But now I was aware. And there was no stopping me.

First, I went vegetarian. Then I started to learn more about veganism and how animals suffered for things like dairy and eggs, so within a 6-month period, I went fully vegan. It took me time to figure out what I'd eat, what it meant for my wider lifestyle (like did I want to send my leather boots to a charity shop? Where could I eat out?), and generally digest it all and talk it over with those closest to me so they could support me (some even joined me!).

It was the best decision I ever made. My past choices to eat meat do not define me. But what I do next does. And I will do everything in my power to end animal suffering.

Although I can't stop all cruelty to living creatures on the planet, I can be kinder to every living creature in my life.

River Phoenix

Vegan rights

The rights of vegans have been recognised in international law since the 1948 Universal Declaration of Human Rights ('the Declaration') was enacted. The rights provided by the Declaration are qualified, meaning signatory nations have discretion as to how they are applied in domestic law. However, the Declaration has still provided a solid foundation on which to develop the rights of vegans in the UK.

For example, in January 2020, Judge Robin Postle ruled that being vegan for ethical reasons constitutes a 'philosophical belief' and as such amounts to a "protected characteristic" under the Equality Act 2010 ("the Act").[27] This landmark ruling significantly changed the landscape for ethical vegans, affording them the same rights as any other "religion or belief" recognised under the Act. The Vegan Society is a great source of information if you'd like to find out more about vegan rights internationally.[28]

Employers' responsibilities

Employers have a responsibility to their staff to ensure that they are not subject to discrimination in the workplace. Vegans can experience discrimination in both direct and indirect ways. An example of direct discrimination could be treating someone less favourably because they're vegan, such as not inviting them to a staff meal. An example of indirect discrimination would be having a policy that puts vegans at a disadvantage, such as a food purchasing policy that does not provide vegan options.

When we talk about discrimination, we consider unconscious bias as well, which includes the associations we hold outside of our consciousness and control. This can come into play with vegans in the workplace in many situations. Maybe colleagues automatically assume you're some sort of eco-terrorist and here to cause a problem or that you are deficient of some essential nutrients? Or maybe you wash less because vegans are hippies? The reality is that with 3% of the world's population being vegan, we come in many different forms, and like with all equality groups, people should check their biases before they lead to discrimination.

If your employer doesn't understand veganism, why not start up a conversation with them about it and see how you can support them in building their awareness and inclusivity? For more information on veganism in the workplace, see the 'Resources' section.

Focus on what's important

Starting out on this journey can seem daunting at first. There's so much information out there, and sometimes the thought of animals suffering may make you want to change everything in your lifestyle overnight.

Stop.

Take a breath.

Focus.

The best place to start is to think about what is most important to you. It's all about making sustainable change, so starting with what you're passionate about will set you in good stead and help you stay focussed on your goals.

Think about your lifestyle. Are you a foodie who loves to cook and wants to understand more about vegan nutrition? Perhaps you love makeup and want to find out if what you are using is cruelty-free? Write down your top three priorities that you want to focus on first in your vegan journey.

My top three priorities

1.

2.

3.

Here's some inspiration if you need it.

1. Learning how to cook my favourite meals vegan
2. Figuring out how to read food labelling and see the hidden ingredients I need to look out for
3. Getting my family and friends on board so they understand why I am vegan
4. Checking if my beauty products are cruelty-free
5. Reading up on vegan literature so I can communicate with others about it

Once you've identified what your priorities are, if you want to jump straight to the section on those topics, head back to the Contents and navigate to where you want to go.

Remember, this isn't about perfectionism. You are at the start of a beautiful journey. You will make mistakes, and that's ok. You'll learn from them and be better for it.

PROGRESS <u>NOT</u> PERFECTION
PROGRESS <u>NOT</u> PERFECTION
PROGRESS <u>NOT</u> PERFECTION
PROGRESS <u>NOT</u> PERFECTION
PROGRESS <u>NOT</u> PERFECTION
PROGRESS <u>NOT</u> PERFECTION
PROGRESS <u>NOT</u> PERFECTION
PROGRESS <u>NOT</u> PERFECTION
PROGRESS <u>NOT</u> PERFECTION

@marieforieo

Pearls of wisdom

When researching to create this journal, a cohort of vegans were surveyed to hear what they wanted to know about when they first went vegan. Their feedback has been woven into the design of this book, but they also left messages and pearls of wisdom they would like to share with aspiring vegans. Here's the best of them.

Disclaimer: You will feel warm and fuzzy inside after reading!

Give up dairy cheese and milk a couple of weeks before trying vegan alternatives, as your taste buds change. It makes the transition easier.

Speak to other vegans. They are happy to help if you have questions, no matter how insignificant you think it might be.

Just do it, you won't regret it!

Do this for yourself, first and foremost. You make a difference; don't worry about everyone else at the start.

Be armed with facts in case people challenge your decision to go vegan. But remember, it's also okay to politely decline to answer.

Make a transition plan and find support.

It's so much easier than you think.

Don't put pressure on yourself to do things perfectly. You'll get things wrong and you'll keep learning. You're doing your best and that's amazing.

Take one step at a time. Each will have a big impact on helping conserve our planet.

You won't make everyone understand or feel the same as you. Keep that in mind before you go in to battle with people!

It will be so worth it, and you'll learn so many new skills.

Embrace new ideas and new foods.

Make connections with others. You don't have to do it alone.

You're doing a great thing. There are so many people and resources waiting to help you.

Start small if you need too. Be patient. It gets so much easier.

You're an awesome human for caring so much!

Don't beat yourself up if you accidentally slip up. Learn and move on.

Don't be put off by other people.

Future visioning

In the spirit of future thinking, one day, you'll be the seasoned vegan. Write down what you envisage future you will look like. What will you be doing? How will your life have changed? Is there anything you'd like to say to future you?

When you lose track and feel lost, come back to this. An added benefit of future visioning is that you are clearly setting your intentions and manifesting the reality you desire.

What does my vegan future look like?

How will my life have changed for the better?

A message that future me would want to give present me.

What difference will I have made in the world?

CHAPTER TWO

FOOD

Each day, a person who eats a vegan diet saves:

1,100 gallons of water
45 pounds of grain
30 sq ft of forested land
20 lbs CO2 equivalent
1 animal's life.

Cowspiracy

Is it from an animal or insect?

Navigating a whole new world of food can be daunting, but once you find your feet with a few basics, you'll be well on your way to being a fully-fledged vegan food expert. The following pages are going to show you how.

For information about why vegans don't eat animals, head to the 'Why go vegan' section.

Depending on where you're at on your vegan journey, you may not be sure which food is or isn't vegan. If that's you, it's all good! Let's clear it up. Essentially, vegans avoid anything that comes from an animal, such as the flesh or any other products they produce (think honey, eggs, milk, etc.).

This little flow chart can be really handy. It's so simple, but it's effective! You can also cut it out and give it to others who might need a helping hand; maybe your friends, partner, or parents who keep asking what you can and can't eat.

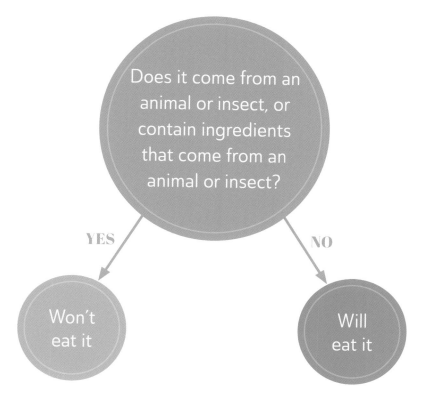

Does it come from an animal or insect, or contain ingredients that come from an animal or insect?

YES

NO

Won't eat it

Will eat it

Nutrients

When you first go vegan, you may feel concerned about where you're getting all your nutrients from, maybe even more so than you were before. Most people are actually healthier when they go vegan because they are thinking more about what goes into their body and often realise that their diet before wasn't sufficient in getting all the goodness they needed anyway.

It's always good to have an understanding of where nutrients come from, but don't feel like you need to stress about how many grams of everything you are getting each day. Just focus on eating a healthy, well-balanced diet and you'll be well on your way to a much healthier lifestyle. Eating a range of colourful fruits and veg, nuts and seeds is helpful in getting all the trace minerals you need.

If you have certain health conditions, please consult a plant-based nutritionist for detailed advice and guidance to make sure you tailor your diet to what's best for your needs. See the 'Resources' section at the end of this book for some recommendations.

Fun fact: There are virtually no nutrients in animal-based foods that are not better provided by plants, which makes plants pretty amazing, right? B12 is the most difficult vitamin to obtain; so many vegans choose to supplement to ensure they get the right amount.

Let's put the archaic stereotype of malnourished vegans to bed once and for all by covering the basics of where you can find some of the most important nutrients.

Protein
Whole grains, nuts, seeds, spinach, broccoli, beans, peas, lentils, peanuts, and soy foods, such as tofu, tempeh, and soy-based vegan meats.

Omega-3 Fatty Acids

Fish are touted as a great source of omega-3s. But did you know that fish get their omegas from eating algae? So can vegans! You can add things like seaweed, nori, and spirulina to dishes. Omega-3 can also be generated from eating chia, hemp seed, flax, and walnuts.

Iron
Beans, soya foods, dried fruit (such as dates, figs, and apricots), nuts and seeds, wholegrain cereals, and green leafy vegetables.

Calcium
Fortified foods, such as plant milks and bread*, beans (e.g., baked, kidney, butter, etc.), lentils, tahini, sesame seeds, and chickpeas (can be in the form of hummus!).

Zinc
Wholegrain cereals, spinach, mushrooms, beans, chickpeas, pumpkin seeds, broccoli, peas, and lentils.

Selenium
Button mushrooms, brown rice, oats, Brazil nuts, and tofu.

Magnesium
Green leafy vegetables, wholegrain cereals, almonds, cashews, and green beans.

Vitamin A
Carrots, green leafy vegetables, red and yellow peppers, romaine lettuce, sweet potatoes, mangoes, and apricots.

Vitamin C
Cauliflower, oranges, red pepper, strawberries, kiwifruit, tomatoes, potatoes, blackcurrants, and papaya.

Vitamin D
Fortified foods, such as plant milks, cereals, and margarines*, and sunlight!

Vitamin E
Spinach, almonds, sunflower seeds, olives, and red peppers.

Vitamin K
Green, leafy vegetables, such as kale, broccoli, sprouts, spinach, and potatoes.

B Vitamins
Mushrooms, bananas, peas, green leafy vegetables, nuts, and avocados.

B12
Fortified foods, such as plant milks*, nutritional yeast flakes, and yeast extracts (such as marmite).

* Check the labels as not all brands are fortified.

Hidden ingredients

Below is a list of ingredients that are not vegan to look out for when food shopping. They can be innocently hidden in ingredients lists and aren't always shown in bold as they may not be allergens.

Why not screenshot or tear this page out and take it with you when shopping so you have the list to hand? Or you could download an app that identifies all the ingredients (a list of recommended apps is in the 'Resources' section).

Ingredient Name(s)	What It Is
Albumin	A binder derived from eggs
Aspic	Thickener usually derived from gelatine
Beeswax, E901	Wax produced by honeybees
Casein	A protein found in milk
Cochineal, Carmine, Natural Red 4, E120, CI 75470	Crushed up female Cochineal beetles
Gelatine, E441	A protein obtained from boiling skin, tendons, ligaments, and/or bones with water
Honey, Royal Jelly	Secretions from bees
Isinglass	Swim bladders of fish
Lactic Acid	Made from Lactose*
Lactose, E966	A sugar present in dairy
Lard	Animal fat
L.cysteine, E910, E920, E921	Often made from human hair or bird feathers*
Lecithin, E322*	Fatty substance from animal tissues
Oleic Acid, Oleinic Acid	Rendered animal fat
Omega-3 fatty acids	Oils from fish*
Rennet	Stomach lining of young goats, calves, and lambs
Shellac, Confectioners Glaze, E904	Hardened secretions from the Lac bug
Suet	Fat taken from the kidneys of sheep and cows*
Tallow	Animal fat
Vitamin D3	Derived from lamb's wool or fish oil
Whey	The liquid that remains after milk has been curdled and strained

*Can also be plant-derived.

Some tips on reading food labelling

> 'Free from' does not mean free from all animal products, e.g., 'free from chicken nuggets' could be free from an allergen like milk but are still made with actual chicken. When shopping in the 'free from' isle, always consider that there may still be animal products present.

> When trying to read food labels quickly (you will become a ninja at this in no time), if it says vegetarian, you'll know that there is no meat present, so you'll only need to skim read for things like milk, eggs, honey, etc.

> Allergens like milk and egg will always be in bold so are easy to spot, but some animal ingredients won't be (honey, I'm looking at you!).

> Be ready to feel incredibly frustrated at the fact that milk powder is in EVERYTHING! Your fellow vegans understand your frustrations!

> 'May contain' will often be present on lots of foods that would otherwise be vegan. It is a personal choice if you want to eat them. Most vegans do because it usually means it has been produced in the same factory as animal products, but they are not an ingredient in the food item itself. Companies use this as a cover all for allergen reasons.

Alcohol is worth mentioning as it surprisingly isn't always vegan. Some wine companies use egg and dairy proteins in the fining process, and impurities in some wines and beers are removed using Isinglass, an ingredient made from the dried swim bladders of fish. There are plenty of vegan-friendly brands out there, and lots of companies now label them as such. Better yet, choosing the vegan versions don't mean forfeiting taste, as these processes are unnecessary and have animal-free counterparts. Cream-based liquors are also ones to watch out for as they can contain dairy.

Swaps

When learning to cook vegan, the art is in finding alternatives and making swaps that taste good to you. Use the next page to write down what swaps you plan to make for your favourite foods. You'll see some examples below to get you going.

Swap for

Scrambled eggs	⟶	Scrambled tofu
Pulled pork	⟶	Jackfruit marinated in BBQ sauce
Tuna mayo	⟶	Tinned vegan tuna alternative. If you're feeling creative, try banana blossom or chickpeas seasoned with seaweed flakes
Creamy milk in hot drinks	⟶	Oat milk
Eggs in baking	⟶	Chia, Aquafaba (juice from chickpeas), apple sauce, or bananas
Beef or chicken burger	⟶	Beef or chicken-style burger (usually made from soya)
White sauce for lasagne	⟶	Vegan white sauce alternative (you can buy it ready made in jars from many large supermarkets). If you're feeling creative, cut and roast butternut squash and then blend with some plant milk and nutritional yeast
Dairy yoghurt	⟶	Coconut or soya alternative

The possibilities are endless, and the more you experiment, the easier it will be to know what you do and don't like, making veganising favourite meals or planning new ones so much easier.

The added benefit is this will ultimately push you out of your comfort zone by trying new foods. Not only will you benefit health-wise, but also flavour and experience wise!

Meat alternatives are very commonplace now, but not all vegans like to eat them. You may be thinking 'why would vegans want to eat something that looks and tastes like meat?' Well, vegans want to eliminate animal suffering, that doesn't by default mean they don't enjoy the taste of meat. Some vegans may also want help transitioning away from meat. Plant-based meat alternatives have a valid place in a vegan world, and it's a personal choice if you want to include them in your diet or not.

Swaps I want to try / swaps I have tried and like:

Swap for

Every small change you make adds up. You're not expected to get this right on day 1.

Sadie Jade

Foods I'd like to try

- [x] e.g., tofu, quinoa, jackfruit
- [ ]
- [ ]
- [ ]
- [ ]
- [ ]
- [ ]
- [ ]
- [ ]
- [ ]
- [ ]
- [ ]

- [ ]
- [ ]
- [ ]
- [ ]
- [ ]
- [ ]
- [ ]
- [ ]
- [ ]
- [ ]
- [ ]

Recipes

Try veganising some of your favourite meals so you have a few in the bank that you know you enjoy. Here's an example to get you started.

Meal: Spaghetti Bolognese

Non-vegan ingredients to swap out:

Swap for

Beef mince	$\longrightarrow$	Diced mushrooms or lentils
Red wine	$\longrightarrow$	Red wine that doesn't contain egg
Dark chocolate	$\longrightarrow$	Dairy-free dark chocolate alternative
Parmesan	$\longrightarrow$	Vegan parmesan or cheese alternative or nutritional yeast
Garlic bread	$\longrightarrow$	Brand that contains no milk or cheese or is homemade using bread crusts, garlic powder, and butter

Any new methods of cooking I need to note:

> Fry off the mushroom before adding it to this dish as it carries excess water.

> Don't need to cook for as long because there is no real meat ingredients. Experiment with how long I like it cooked for to bring out the flavours and burn off any alcohol in the wine.

Notes / findings:

> Needed to cook for at least 30 minutes.

> Would probably add some frozen vegan mince as well as the mushrooms next time for texture.

> Tastes better the second day!

Meal:

Non-vegan ingredients to swap out:

Swap for

	→
	→
	→
	→
	→

Any new methods of cooking I need to note:

Notes / findings:

Meal: _____

Non-vegan ingredients to swap out:

Swap for

	→	
	→	
	→	
	→	
	→	

Any new methods of cooking I need to note:

_____
_____
_____
_____

Notes / findings:

_____
_____
_____
_____

Meal:

Non-vegan ingredients to swap out:

Swap for

	$\longrightarrow$	
	$\longrightarrow$	
	$\longrightarrow$	
	$\longrightarrow$	
	$\longrightarrow$	

Any new methods of cooking I need to note:

Notes / findings:

Doing the food shop

Eating vegan is often misconceived as being more expensive, when in reality, it can be the cheaper option. Fresh fruits and veg, and things like rice and pasta, are all relatively low cost, especially when compared to meat or dairy. There are higher priced vegan items available, but these would be considered luxury items (the same as meat) and not essential to leading a healthy vegan diet.

When shopping, you may like to support local where you can, say from a fruit and veg market or green grocers if you have one close by. This helps support small businesses, can reduce your carbon footprint if they are growing their own veg that hasn't travelled thousands of miles to get to you, and will also be in keeping with eating seasonally.

However, inevitably, you might need to visit supermarkets sometimes, and it's worth having an idea of how to navigate them as a vegan (yes, this is a thing). If you're new to the vegan shopping game, when you first walk into any supermarket it can feel a little overwhelming now that there are whole isles of foods that you no longer want to eat. Here are some essential tips to help you shop successfully:

> Before you go, do a quick online search to see what vegan food the supermarket of your choice offers. One might appeal more to you than another.

> Find some blogs or social media pages that share where you can buy different vegan foods. They'll help you identify accidentally vegan products as well (products that weren't intended to be vegan but are).

> Go to the shop with a list and categorise it into sections, so you don't need to do too many laps trying to find things (e.g., dried goods, chilled, frozen).

> 'Free from' isles will be where you'll find specialist items, like vegan chocolate, custard, sauces, etc.; however, vegan products are becoming more part of the overall supermarket layout now, so you'll often find vegan cheese in an isle next to the dairy cheeses. The same goes for fake meats and ice cream.

You might not be able to get everything you need from one place, depending on where you live and what you like to eat. As you learn which vegan alternatives float your boat, you might find that you prefer the own brand cheese from one shop and the biscuits from another. If this is the case, try to plan a visit to certain shops when you're in the area, if it's just to pick up a few things, or alternate the shops each week. If one is a little further away, maybe clear a cupboard or shelf so you can store a little supply of your faves to keep you going for a while.

> Use the next page to keep a track of those favourite vegan items and where you can find them.

Also, food shopping for vegans can sometimes be an unpleasant experience when faced with isles of body parts and products made from the suffering of animals. Here's what some vegans say about their experiences of the meat isle:

> "I feel a heaviness of heart knowing what those animals went through to end up shrink-wrapped and in that fridge."

> "I just want to run around telling everyone what happens behind closed doors to these once beautiful, gentle, sentient beings."

> "It can be a bit distressing. Sometimes I just want to cry."

You may not experience these feelings, but if you do, know that it is completely normal and you are not alone. Reach out to those close to you or perhaps those in your vegan community for support (see the 'Community' section for more advice on this).

Sometimes your favourite vegan foods will be spread out across various shops. Keep track of them all here.

Favourite vegan item	Shop I can find it in

Meal planning

Planning is the key to success!

Use the following pages to map out what you plan to eat throughout the week to help you feel prepared and in control. Having a plan will stop you feeling lost in a sea of decisions and information and will help you learn, bit by bit, what you can and can't eat. If you want more blank meal plans, feel free to photocopy the page so you have an unlimited supply!

If you have some days when you'll be away from home and think you'll have limited food choices, having a plan can reassure you that you won't be caught hungry. Packed lunch is a life saver!

Start by looking for vegan recipes and meal ideas, either in books or online, searching for foods you enjoy or want to try, and start veganising your favourite recipes (see the 'Food' chapter for templates).

> A top tip from seasoned vegans is to not overload yourself with lots of new foods to try all in one go. Spread things out so you have time and the head space to really experience them.

An added benefit of meal planning is less food waste. A study in the US showed that the average household wasted about a third of the food they purchased,[29] and the UN estimate that 11% of all global food produced is wasted by households.[30] If you're planning ahead, you can make sure you factor in meals that use up that whole punnet of mushrooms or bag of kale you brought. Less waste also means less money lost in fruit and veg that's spoiled in the fridge.

Weekly meal planner

	Breakfast	Lunch	Dinner	Snack
Monday				
Tuesday				
Wednesday				
Thursday				
Friday				
Saturday				
Sunday				

Shopping list

- [x] e.g., tofu, quinoa, jackfruit
- [ ]
- [ ]
- [ ]
- [ ]
- [ ]
- [ ]
- [ ]
- [ ]
- [ ]
- [ ]
- [ ]
- [ ]
- [ ]
- [ ]
- [ ]
- [ ]
- [ ]
- [ ]
- [ ]
- [ ]
- [ ]
- [ ]

- [ ]
- [ ]
- [ ]
- [ ]
- [ ]
- [ ]
- [ ]
- [ ]
- [ ]
- [ ]
- [ ]
- [ ]
- [ ]
- [ ]
- [ ]
- [ ]
- [ ]
- [ ]
- [ ]
- [ ]

Weekly meal planner

	Breakfast	Lunch	Dinner	Snack
Monday				
Tuesday				
Wednesday				
Thursday				
Friday				
Saturday				
Sunday				

Shopping list

- ☑ e.g., tofu, quinoa, jackfruit
- ◯
- ◯
- ◯
- ◯
- ◯
- ◯
- ◯
- ◯
- ◯
- ◯
- ◯
- ◯
- ◯
- ◯
- ◯
- ◯
- ◯
- ◯
- ◯
- ◯
- ◯

- ◯
- ◯
- ◯
- ◯
- ◯
- ◯
- ◯
- ◯
- ◯
- ◯
- ◯
- ◯
- ◯
- ◯
- ◯
- ◯
- ◯
- ◯
- ◯
- ◯
- ◯
- ◯

Weekly meal planner

	Breakfast	Lunch	Dinner	Snack
Monday				
Tuesday				
Wednesday				
Thursday				
Friday				
Saturday				
Sunday				

Shopping list

- [x] e.g., tofu, quinoa, jackfruit

Eating out

Navigating eating out is a whole new experience as a vegan. Although 100% vegan restaurants are popping up all over the world, there will inevitably be instances where you are eating somewhere that may have limited options. Here are a few tips for making it a smooth and enjoyable experience.

> - Look online at menus before heading out for dinner to get an idea of their vegan options. You might need to mix and match certain dishes if they have really poor options (at this point, if you can, find another place to eat!).
>
> - If you think your friends or family don't understand your dietary preferences, offer to book the restaurant so you can call ahead and chat with the restaurant directly about your requirements.
>
> - When talking to restaurant staff, if they aren't aware of what vegan is, be prepared with how you would like to explain your dietary choice, e.g., I don't eat anything from an animal, which includes things like their flesh, milk, eggs, and cheese.

When thinking about where to eat, some vegans choose to avoid certain chains or restaurants because of the way they treat animals, even if they have vegan options available (e.g., fast food chains and their reputation for animal cruelty and intensive farming). However, some vegans believe that when eating at these places, it shows them what people want, that we are demanding the future by paying for vegan options and this directly influences restaurants to change to meet the preferences of its customers.

Some vegans do not like to eat at the same table with people who are eating animals, while others feel that mealtimes are an opportunity to convert their meat-eating friends or family and that avoiding eating with them sends the wrong impression of veganism (unfortunately, not everyone is sympathetic to the fact that seeing dead animals can be upsetting for some vegans). Each person is different, and it's up to you to decide what feels most comfortable for you.

In the spirit of preparedness, take the opportunity to think about the places you like to eat out. Consider their vegan food offerings and then look into the way they do business (e.g. ethical, sustainable). Does it fit with your morals and values?

Does it fit with my morals and values?

(Circle the smiley that applies)

Places I like to eat out at:

Yes 😊 Kind of 😐 No 🙁

Food shouldn't cost the earth

Palm oil has been and continues to be a major driver of deforestation of some of the world's most biodiverse forests, destroying the habitat of already endangered species, such as the orangutan, pygmy elephant, and Sumatran rhino. Forests are destroyed to make way for palm plantations, and often the methods used to clear land is via uncontrolled fires. As you can imagine, this devastates the landscape, wildlife, and air quality.

Palm oil is a highly useful, edible vegetable oil that comes from the fruit of oil palm trees and is present in many of the pre-packaged food products that we buy at the supermarket, such as pizza, doughnuts, biscuits, and chocolate.

Food aside, palm oil can even be found in products such as deodorant, shampoo, toothpaste, and lipstick. It's also used in animal feed and as a biofuel in many parts of the world (not in the UK though!).

For these reasons, some vegans will try to avoid palm oil wherever possible.

CHAPTER THREE

LIFESTYLE

Fashion

When shopping for clothes and accessories, keep in mind that some designers still use materials from animals, such as fur, leather, silk, or wool.

Animals farmed for fashion live miserable lives, often in cramped conditions, and face unthinkable suffering when they are killed for their pelts. We usually just think of cows being killed for their skin as a waste product of the meat industry, but the leather industry is much bigger in comparison. Dogs are also killed for their skin and can be sold as 'leather', so you might not actually be buying cow hide! In some of the countries that are the biggest producers of leather, cows and dogs have been filmed being skinned alive, which is not uncommon practice.

Similarly, wild animals like coyotes that are caught and killed for their fur can suffer for days in snares or traps waiting to be collected, some even starving or bleeding to death.

Snakes, crocodiles, lizards, and frogs are harvested for their skins to be made into shoes, handbags, and other exotic leather items. Even oysters are exploited and killed for their pearls.

Some ethical vegans will still buy from suppliers that also sell animal products and believe that, in buying ethical choices from a retailer, they are informing demand with their money. Others, however, will try to boycott them altogether. But access to money plays a part in where people are able to shop and what they can afford; it doesn't always come down to just ethics.

When thinking about replacing animal products with alternatives, some vegans will want to consider the environmental impact that their replacement counterparts have, such as replacing a wool jumper for one made from cheap synthetic materials that won't last as long and will end up in landfill quickly.

A few tips to help you shop savvy and reduce your impact are:

> Buy pre-loved second-hand

> Invest in items that will stand the test of time

> Go to clothes swap events

> Mend old clothing where possible (this not only saves you from buying more but saves on landfill too!)

Fast fashion outlets often have a huge impact on the environment for many reasons, not just the obvious use of cheap materials that don't last. Shockingly, a large number of clothes that are returned end up in landfill. This is because companies don't have the production mechanisms in place to be able to process the returns in the many different ways needed. It is more cost-effective to just dispose of them.[31]

Have a think about where you buy your clothing from and then do a quick online search to find out if those brands or outlets are squeaky clean or in fact have a dark side that doesn't fit with your values.

Brand/designer/ outlet	Contains animal products in some or all of their lines	Has a bad environmental footprint	Will I continue to buy from them?
Designer X	Yes – fur and leather are key pieces in a lot of their lines	Yes – mass-produced plastic clothing and bad working conditions!	No
Outlet Y	Yes – some leather shoes and belts	Unsure – not much info available	Yes – cost-effective for me and not a huge animal-based line (few leather belts)

Tip: Lots of prominent animal rights organisations have already done lots of background research on suppliers to save you time and effort. All you have to do is search something like, 'is [brand name] vegan and cruelty free?', and you'll be presented with lots of results. Some popular sites are also recommended in the 'Resources' section.

If you ever wanted Willy to escape in Free Willy,

or the chickens to escape the farmer's pot in Chicken Run,

or you felt incredibly sad for the animals in Babe,

you already understand veganism.

Gift-buying guide

As a vegan, you may not want to use any of your money to buy those you love non-vegan gifts (say goodbye to milk chocolate!). It's really easy to find gifts that align with your values but will also still be amazing for those receiving them.

Here are a few ideas:

> Cruelty-free beauty products

> Vegan chocolate

> A relaxing treatment at a salon that uses cruelty-free products

> Clothing from sustainable suppliers

> Sponsor an animal or make a donation to a sanctuary in their name

> Make them something if you're feeling crafty

> A re-useable water bottle or travel mug

> Put together a hamper with some vegan products they will love. Many chutneys and wines are vegan, and you can also fill it with locally sourced fresh foods

> Wallets or purses, shoes, bags, or belts made from leather alternatives. There are so many cool and quirky options now, from leaf leather to mushroom leather!

> Buy merchandise from an organisation you support (lots of animal rights organisations have chocolate, diaries, calendars, etc.)

> Vegan-certified alcohol.

Entertainment

Animals are still exploited for entertainment all over the world every single day. Horses and dogs are shot and killed when they become injured or are generally no longer useful to the racing industry, and some countries still have live animals in circuses or keep elephants in captivity, away from their families, so that humans can ride them. Even some places that we think might be a great haven for animals can be very different behind the scenes, such as zoos and aquariums, where animals may have been brutally captured from the wild or bred to draw in human visitors, often leading miserable lives in small, unnatural enclosures.

Put a cross in any of the boxes below next to activities you currently enjoy.

This is to get you thinking about areas of your social life you may like to change and what you might like to do instead.

- ◯ Horse racing
- ◯ Circuses (with animals)
- ◯ Aquarium
- ◯ Fishing
- ◯ Dog racing
- ◯ Zoo
- ◯ Hunting or shooting
- ◯ Dolphin or whale shows
- ◯ Animal rides (e.g., donkeys/elephants/horses)
- ◯ TV and media using animals in adverts, films, or shows

Thoughts on alternative things I might like to try instead (e.g., visiting sanctuaries that rescue animals):

Waste

Everything we consume has to go somewhere, right? Landfills and waste deposited into the ocean is destroying habitats at an alarming rate, with some studies now showing disastrous effects on marine life, such as plastic present in the stomachs of whales and fish.

Here are a few things you might like to do to think about reducing or recycling your waste.

Tick them off as you do them (or before if you're already there!).

○ Check out your local waste collection. What can and can't they recycle? (Have you been putting food waste in the wrong bin or thinking cling film can be recycled?).

○ Consider other things you're throwing away that could be saved and recycled during a trip to your local recycling centre (e.g., tetra cartons and carrier bags).

○ Try to cut down on food waste. Plan your meals as much as possible to use up food.

○ Look into composting methods that are accessible to you (e.g., bokashi for those needing space-saving methods).

○ Invest in a reusable water bottle or coffee cup.

○ Choose waste-free options where possible (e.g., loose fruit and veg, not in plastic packaging).

○ Stop using single use plastic wherever possible (e.g., select bagless when shopping online if they have the option).

○ Don't put harsh substances down the drain, such as paints or stripping agents. Dispose of them correctly at waste processing plants (or better yet, buy eco-versions).

○ Donate good condition unwanted clothing, toys, or household items to charity rather than disposing of them.

Travel

When planning your holidays and travelling as a vegan, there are a few things to consider.

There are lots of blogs out there to help you plan your trips, but here are the most common things to think about.

Places to stay

Exclusive vegan boutiques and hotels are starting to pop up all over the world, which make for the most hassle-free stay but can come with a price tag to match, so you'll need to be thrifty to find well-priced locations. Lots of non-vegan specific hotels are starting to cater for vegans when it comes to food in their restaurants, but if in doubt, many are usually happy to exchange emails before you book to confirm how they can accommodate you. There are areas of the world that are more vegan savvy than others, so it's best to check. Alternatively, you can book privately-rented accommodation and self-cater.

If staying somewhere where toiletries are supplied, check ahead if they are cruelty free or pack your own to avoid the issue altogether.

Getting there

Some people, predominantly those who have gone vegan for environmental reasons, may have committed to 'no-fly', which means they will not travel anywhere by aeroplane because of the emissions linked to this form of transport. Even if you don't commit to no-fly, looking at how you travel and ways you may be able to minimise environmental impact, such as using public transport, is worth considering.

Eating vegan

Before travelling, have a browse online at what's local and view some menus or look at recommendations from other vegans on where to eat. Someone has usually done the hard graft in researching for you! You can also download or buy vegan translation sheets to take with you that explain your dietary preferences in case language is a barrier when ordering food.

Avoiding exploitation

Package holidays often come with added excursions or day trips. Be mindful of booking on any that include things like trips to Sea World or zoos or animal rides, such as on elephants or camels.

Planning my next holiday

Use this page to plan your next trip, making note of all your essential pre-holiday research.

Am I committing to no-fly?   ◯ Yes   ◯ No

Holiday destinations: 1.
                        2.
                        3.

Accommodation plans

Vegan food available at my destination

Public transport/low carbon travel options

Activities/plans while I'm there

Since going vegan, I feel so at peace.

I now live my life true to my values because I love animals and no longer contribute to their suffering.

Michelle (Sadie's mum)

Children

Whether you already have children or would like them in the future, use this page to get to grips with navigating the world of vegan parenting.

Growing gains

It is completely possible and beneficial to raise children on a vegan diet. They will, if anything, be healthier for it. Just make sure you are giving them a large variety of fresh fruit and vegetables. You can seek the advice of a plant-based nutritionist or paediatrician if you'd like more professional guidance. There are also lots of online communities run by and for parents of vegan children that can help get you started and that provide inspiration and support.

Enabling choice

Choosing to raise your children vegan can draw judgement from others who may think you are forcing your beliefs onto your kids, or who might not understand that a vegan diet is actually much healthier for them. Most people, yourself included no doubt, have been raised to think we need meat, eggs, and dairy to be healthy.

A good way to approach these situations is to politely explain that choosing to raise your child vegan is no different to a parent choosing to feed their children animal products. You are simply making a choice (if they are too young to choose themselves) that is in their best interest to keep them healthy, as you know that eating animal products can lead to multiple diseases and health issues. Also, most kids, if you actually ask them, wouldn't want an animal to be hurt, so you're probably more in keeping with their wishes than parents choosing to feed their kids animal products! This can be a dicey subject to talk about with other parents, so choose your words wisely. You want to help them understand, not walk away feeling attacked or belittled (even if that is what they tried to do to you in the first place!). You're better than that.

Socialising

When your kids get to a certain age, they'll no doubt be invited to lots of birthday parties. Often, your child will be faced with non-vegan party food options, so plan how you'd like to approach this. Some vegan parents are okay with telling their children why they eat vegan at home but are happy for them to make the choice themselves when they are away from home, whereas others like to prepare food to send with their child so that they have vegan options. Speak to the hosting parent beforehand so they understand your situation and can help to make your child feel included in the celebrations rather than an outsider with a 'special' plate. Most people are willing and happy to accommodate if you explain things to them.

Pets

Deciding whether to keep pets or not is a personal choice, and vegans can differ on where they sit on the topic. There are beliefs held by some vegans that animals are not meant for human ownership and they therefore choose not to keep them, while others believe that humans and some animals can co-exist and form beautiful bonds and relationships. Additionally, there are millions of domestic animals that have been bred into existence that need homes and couldn't survive in the wild, so some vegans would choose to adopt and not shop for specifically bred pets.

Breeding

Breeding domestic animals for pets presents a few issues.

> They often have health issues due to inbreeding or selective breeding for 'desirable' traits, which cause them discomfort and pain (e.g., pugs with breathing problems due to a squashed nose).

> There are little to no regulations around checking the credentials of the buyer, so animals could end up with unsuitable owners.

> Animals become profitable and are therefore seen as commodities. This also feeds into the pet theft trade for more expensive breeds.

> There are many homeless animals left in shelters that are just as worthy and deserving of a good home but get overlooked because of the misconception that they are there because they are damaged goods or because their breed is misunderstood.

Feeding

What we feed our companion animals can be tricky for a person who wants to avoid animal exploitation wherever practicably possible yet may need to buy animal-based pet food. Research suggests that "both cats and dogs may thrive on vegetarian diets"[32] so long as they are nutritionally complete and reasonably balanced, so this is a valid option for vegan pet owners.

Like humans, dogs are omnivores, so can eat both plants and meat.[32] In particular, they have been proven to thrive on a plant-based diet, even showing better allergy control, improved weight management, coat condition, arthritis regression, cataract resolution, and overall health and vitality.[33] Vegan dog food is supplemented with the nutrients they need, and you can also feed them a huge range of plant-based foods to keep them healthy.

Cats, on the other hand, are obligate carnivores, meaning they rely on meat for their nutrients. Vegan cat food is supplemented with the nutrients they need to be healthy, but unlike dogs, there are fewer foods they can tolerate. There are many examples of healthy vegan cats though, so it's well worth doing your research to see what you feel is best for your feline friend.

Lifestyles

Vegans (and non-vegans!) want to give their companion animals happy lives. This might sometimes mean that they have to make decisions in their animals' best interests, even if they have to go against their beliefs, e.g., to buy their cat meat products.

Vegans would potentially not own exotic animals or birds. They are notoriously hard to keep because recreating their complex natural conditions is often impossible in captivity and exotics need to be fed live or dead animals, like mice or insects. However, if an exotic animal is being rehomed, a vegan may consider giving it a good life and a loving home.

Vegan is just pure love. Love for animals, love for the planet, and love for yourself.

Mischa Temaul

CHAPTER FOUR

PERSONAL CARE

Animal experiments

This section is all about personal care, which can range from the cosmetics and products we use to our health care and medications.

Sadly, animals are used to test the safety of many products and for medical research purposes, which can be extremely distressing and harrowing for them. The variation of animals used is vast but includes mostly mice and rats because they are small, cheap, and easy to breed. But guinea pigs, rabbits, cats, dogs, monkeys, birds, reptiles, pigs, sheep, cows, chickens, horses, and fish are also routinely used.

The government defines an animal experiment as a procedure that is 'likely to cause ... pain, suffering, distress, or lasting harm'. Laboratory animals are typically kept in small cages or kennels and often denied any comfort or stimulation. Until they are killed at the end of the experiment, which could last days, weeks, months, or even years, their lives are often marked by pain and fear, deprived of the ability to exercise any of their natural instincts and stressed due to the frustration of confinement.

In the UK, around four million animals are used in laboratory experiments each year. Hundreds of thousands more animals are bred and killed so that parts of their bodies can be used in research. In addition, millions of surplus animals are bred but never used – they are just disposed of and their deaths are not even recorded.

Here are a few common ways in which animals are used in experiments:

> Irritation tests, where chemicals are rubbed into patches of shaved skin or eyes of restrained animals that have not been given pain relief.

> To test new drugs or surgical techniques for medical research, animals are surgically damaged, given cancer, infected with viruses, brain damaged, and injured in other ways in an attempt to recreate human diseases.

> During 'lethal dose' tests, an animal is forced to consume large amounts of a chemical to determine the dose that causes death.

> At the end of the experiment, animals are often killed by having their necks broken, suffocation, or decapitation.

The number of genetically modified (GM) animals is increasing rapidly. This is the process of specifically either breeding animals with genes added or removed to cause abnormalities or deformities or ensuring that animals will develop certain diseases, like cancer. For every GM mouse used in an experiment, hundreds more die or are killed, either because they are surplus to requirements, because they fail to exhibit the desired genetic alteration, or because they are born with other unintended malformations.

Thankfully, there are many innovative and cruelty-free methods of research available now that can easily and more effectively replace animal testing, such as human cell-based trials, and sophisticated computer models, alongside a whole history of safe ingredients that we already know much about. These methods are even shown to provide more reliable results overall and cause zero suffering.

With special thanks to Animal Aid for the above information.[34]

Never believe that
animals suffer
less than humans.
Pain is the same
for them that it is
for us. Even worse,
because they cannot
help themselves.

Louis J. Camuti

Medication

Animals are used for creating medicines in three ways:

1. **To trial new drugs.**

2. **To help find cures and prevent diseases.**

3. **For ingredients, such as milk or body parts.**

Veganism is about eliminating the exploitation of animals as much as is practicably possible, but we can't be perfect all the time. Some people will need to and should use necessary medications; looking after our health is as much a priority as ending animal exploitation. When we are well, we are able to continue being effective advocates for a better world.

You could help support your overall health with natural remedies where you can, such as magnesium and hot baths for muscle pains, peppermint oil for headaches, and ginger for nausea. The natural world holds many healing powers to help keep us well. But please do not avoid seeking a medical professional's guidance for health concerns when advice is required.

As well as natural remedies, you can try choosing medications that don't contain animal ingredients where you can, such as looking for pain killers that aren't gelatine-coated. It may not always be possible to avoid as sometimes the tablets we need for certain conditions are our only options, but when you have a choice, here are the top non-vegan ingredients to look out for:

Medication Name(s)	What It Is
Gelatine	Made from pig skin, bovine hide, pork, and cattle bones. Used in many medicine capsules
Glycerol	May be derived from animal fats
Lactose	From cows' milk. A common filler in tablets
Lanolin	Fat extracted from sheep's wool
Oleic oil and oleostearin	Made from pressed tallow (fatty substance from boiled cow carcasses)
Shellac	Insect secretion
Stearic acid	Fat from cows, sheep, dogs, or cats. Can be obtained from vegetable sources instead
Trypsin	Enzyme from pork pancreas

Source: Queensland Health.[35]

Vaccines

Vaccines can be a complex area for vegans due to the way the virus used in the vaccine is grown, the ingredients used within the overall vaccine, and the animal testing that takes place before the final product is licenced. It is a personal choice to have a vaccination and you should do what is best for you. This page is given as an educational tool as to the origins and background of vaccinations, not as a deterrent.

Growing the virus

Vaccines are usually made by growing cultures of the target virus or bacterium in cell lines derived from mammals, including humans. These cell lines have been harvested and replicated again and again for ongoing use.

The cell lines used to grow the virus will derive from a primary culture of cells from an organ of a single animal, which has then been propagated repeatedly in the laboratory, often over many decades. For example, the measles vaccine is grown in chick embryo cells and polio vaccines are grown in a mouse cell line. Another animal cell line, now being used to make egg-free flu vaccines, was derived in 1958 from the kidney of a cocker spaniel.

The best-known human cell line is MRC5; these cells derive from the lung of a 14-week-old male foetus from a pregnancy that was terminated for medical reasons in 1966. This cell line is used to grow viruses for vaccines against rubella, chickenpox, and hepatitis A.

Other foetal cell lines, collected in the 1970s and 1980s, have been used for other vaccines, including influenza and some of the new COVID-19 vaccines. No foetal material is present in the final vaccine.

Source: GOV.UK: Guide to the use of human and animal products in vaccines.[36]

Animal ingredients and testing

Animal-derived ingredients can be used in the making of vaccines and as an additive in the final finished product. Some of the most common ingredients are listed on the next page, but the two most commonly used are gelatine (boiled animal body parts) and squalene (oil from shark's liver).

Any new vaccine is currently required in law to be tested on animals before use on humans.

Vivisection

NOUN

The practice of performing operations on live animals for the purpose of experimentation or scientific research.

Oxford Languages

Cosmetics

In the cosmetics industry, animal-derived ingredients are everywhere. From crushed beetles in lipstick, to ground up nails and horns in hair care. Here's a list of everything you need to look out for.

Ingredient	What it is	Which products it's often found in
Ambergris	Derived from the waxy oil that lines the stomachs of whales	Used as a fixative ingredient in expensive perfumes
Carmine (also known as cochineal extract, natural red 4, or CI 75470)	A dye derived from crushing the bodies of female cochineal beetles	Lipsticks and blush products
Collagen*	A protein found mostly in hair, skin, nails, bones, and ligaments of animals	Lip-plumping glosses and anti-aging products
Elastin*	Derived from animal connective tissue	Skincare
Gelatine, E441	Similar to Tallow, gelatine is the boiled skin, ligaments, tendons, and bones of animals	Cream-based skin products and nail treatments
Glycerol*, E422	Rendered animal fat	Toothpaste, hair treatments, cosmetics, and moisturisers
Guanine	A crystalline material that shimmers and/or is light-diffusing, derived from crushed fish scales	Lipsticks, nail polish, and mascara
Honey, Royal Jelly	Substance made by bees from the sugary secretions of plants	Skin and hair care products
Keratin*	Protein made from ground up hair, nails, wool, and horns of animals	Hair care products
Lactose*	Derived from cows' or goats' milk	Skincare products
Lanolin, E913	Fat derived from the grease in sheep's wool	Make-up removers and lipsticks
Tallow	Derived from boiling cow carcasses until a fatty substance is produced	Eye makeup, lipsticks, and foundations
Snail gel	Mucous-like secretion from snails	Skincare and anti-aging products
Squalene	Sourced by squeezing oil from the liver of a shark	Lipsticks and eye makeup products

*Can also be plant-derived.

Animal testing for cosmetics

Many companies may have vegan formulas, but in order to sell cosmetics in certain countries, they have to put their products through animal testing. From March 2013, testing cosmetic products and ingredients on animals was banned within the European Union, but there are claims that this practice is still happening under loopholes in legislation. It's a complex area, and depending on where you live in the world, regulations vary, so it's worth doing your homework on your specific location.

Where I live:

The regulations on animal testing for cosmetics in my country states:

Cosmetics top tips

☆ Be sure to check that products are listed as vegan AND cruelty-free. In the cosmetics world, if something is labelled as vegan, it means it has no animal products in it but does not guarantee it has not been tested on animals.

Just remember:

> **Vegan** = contains no animal products

> **Vegetarian** = doesn't contain animal body parts but may contain some animal products, such as honey, beeswax, or milk

> **Cruelty-free** = not tested on animals, but could contain animal products

☆ You can make some pretty amazing beauty products at home if you want to go that extra step in being completely cruelty-free, and you'll have the added benefit of avoiding putting any bad chemicals on your skin or down the drain as they contain all-natural, harm-free ingredients.

We often already have lots of the components we need to make homemade beauty products in our cupboards. And if we don't, they are relatively cheap and easily accessible. Some of the most commonly used are:

> Apple cider vinegar   > Coconut oil   > Witch Hazel

> Baking soda   > Oats   > Shea butter

> Castile soap   > Salt   > Essential oils

> Tea (usually green, white, and black as they contain antioxidants)

If you want to give homemade beauty a go, start saving up your used bottles and containers so you can re-purpose them. There are plenty of homemade beauty blogs out there sharing tried and tested recipes to get you started.

☆ Essential oils have huge benefits in the realm of beauty and cosmetics. Not only do they smell incredible, they also help with physical and emotional health. It's important to make sure you use pure oils, as synthetic oils will contain chemicals and have none of the natural benefit of the oil.

How to know if your essential oil is pure:

> Check the label. If it says 'pure', you should be ok, but if it says 'perfumed oil', this means it contains synthetic ingredients.

> Pure oils are usually stored in dark glass bottles, coloured amber or blue, as this protects them from ultraviolet damage. Avoid anything that comes in plastic.

☆ Swap out plastic cosmetic items for more eco-friendly versions, like bamboo toothbrushes and sponges. Swap shaving foams and disposable plastic razors for shaving cream bars and recyclable, bladed razors.

☆ Ditch single-use products, like wipes, and replace them with re-useable alternatives to save on the waste you send to landfill. Most wet wipes aren't biodegradable, so it could take 100 years or more for them to breakdown. Even worse, all too often people flush wipes down the toilet so they end up clogging up sewers, damaging marine life and littering beaches.

☆ Opt for false lashes or make-up brushes that are animal fur free (lashes can be made from mink and brushes from animal hair).

☆ Some companies choose not to be certified by recognised organisations, such as Leaping Bunny or The Vegan Society, to show they are vegan or cruelty-free, but it doesn't by default mean they aren't vegan-friendly. If you can't see a logo, look at the company's website or packaging for their commitment statement on animal testing.

☆ Some toilet paper is not vegan-friendly because it contains gelatine, which comes from the bones and skin of animals, or stearic acid, which is animal fat, used to glue the paper fibres together. Always double check the company's processes.

☆ Not all hairdressers use cruelty-free dyes and hair products. Check out what suppliers they use before booking.

Pretty perfect?

Raid through all the products you use, from deodorant to shampoo, and find out how cruelty-free or vegan-friendly they really are. You'll feel amazing with all that knowledge about what you're using and what you might want to replace!

Keep in mind that, if you discover something you own is not vegan-friendly, you may still want to finish using it to avoid excess waste.

Product	Contains animal products?	Tested on animals?	Notes of potential replacements if needed
Shampoo	No	Yes	Switch to a bar that is cruelty-free and saves on plastic

Product	Contains animal products?	Tested on animals?	Notes of potential replacements if needed

Periods

For those who menstruate, if you're wondering how you can have an environmentally-friendly and cruelty-free period, there are three key areas to consider; testing on animals, chemicals, and waste.

Animal testing

If you follow an ethical vegan lifestyle, you will naturally avoid using or purchasing anything that has exploited an animal in any way, which includes the testing of products before they reach our shelves.

A little fact uncommonly known is that some tampon brands have (and in some cases still do) tested on animals. Experiments in the past have included horrific procedures, such as leaving bacteria-laden tampons inside the vaginas of rabbits, baboons, or guinea pigs for extended periods of time to measure the impact of toxic shock syndrome[37] or implanting diffusion chambers into rabbits uteruses, releasing toxins directly into their wombs. These chambers are then retrieved by dissection upon the rabbit's death (caused by the toxins), or 14 days later, they are killed, and it is extracted. These are just two examples of what animals have endured for sanitary product testing.

Another element to consider is that, sometimes, the parent company of the sanitary towel brand may test on animals for other products that they market. Some vegans would rather avoid those organisations altogether, even if the specific sanitary items aren't tested on animals.

You can check out if the company you buy your favourite sanitary items from is ethical. There are so many handy websites out there now to help you find cruelty-free brands. Some of the main ones are:

> Cruelty Free International Leaping Bunny Programme

> PETA   > Cruelty-Free Kitty

The dirty truth

Aside from animal testing, sanitary products can contain harmful chemicals and bleaching agents, described perfectly by Bitesize Vegan as "little toxic seeds of vaginal destruction".[37] These chemicals have no place in products that go anywhere near the most sensitive part of a person's body. Companies are not even required to disclose their ingredients, so there's no easy way of knowing exactly what these products contain.[38] Some feminine wipes also contain strong perfumes that can be extremely irritating to the skin. The best way to avoid contact with toxins is to try out eco-friendly options as they usually also emit the harmful chemicals (see below).

Be enviromenstrually savvy

Being vegan doesn't just stop at wanting to end the senseless testing on animals, it also means protecting our wildlife and oceans. With that in mind, it's important to note that disposable sanitary products, just like nappies, have a huge impact on our environment, and in the US alone, around 12 billion pads and 7 billion tampons are thrown out every year.[39] When you consider all that waste and add the fact that the plastic and non-compostable materials in period products take between 500 to 800 years to decompose,[37] it's a pretty scary thought!

Fortunately, there are environmentally-friendly options available, they just take a little adjusting too. But it's safe to say, once you try them, you'll never look back, and you'll feel so good every cycle knowing you've saved all that waste from landfill.

Some items can cost a little more upfront, but the money you will save over time will be well worth the investment, let alone the benefits to your body and the planet.

Examples of the eco-friendly options available:

> Re-useable sanitary towels that are washable in your machine

> A menstrual cup (for those who prefer tampons)

> Biodegradable disposable pads that don't contain any plastics or chemicals

> Period underwear (looks and feels like normal underwear but has a special layer to prevent blood leaking through)

> Free bleeding (the art of not using any sanitary products at all; most popular on the lighter bleed days or when you can stay home in clothes that you don't mind bleeding on)

Some of these items, like the re-useable sanitary towels and the underwear, will often have a small plastic element to them which ensures they are leak proof. You can source sanitary towels that don't contain plastic, but keep in mind, you may need to change them more regularly to prevent any blood spotting through. Those who want to avoid plastic altogether can also opt for the menstrual cup or free bleeding options. Some vegans are happy to accept the small amount of plastic as they will use the pads for many years to come, but others want to omit it altogether. It's a personal choice and also comes down to what you're able to afford or are comfortable using (e.g., some people may prefer external sanitary wear rather than inserting a menstrual cup so will accept a small amount of plastic present in the pad or pants lining).

When it comes to shopping for eco-friendly period wear, it's best to find some blogs of those who've tried, tested, and recommend different brands. Eco-friendly period wear comes in a huge range of shapes, sizes, and fabrics, so researching the best fit for you will save you money in the long run.

A tip for those who haven't yet made the switch to eco-period wear, try not to use more products than you need by changing your sanitary wear regularly enough to stay clean, but not more than necessary. It seems so simple, but over time, it will reduce the amount of waste you produce.

Eco-period checklist

Look into the credentials of your current period wear (e.g., does the manufacturer test on animals? Are there plastics in the products you use?)

AVOID IN FUTURE! ◯   Phew, they're safe. ◯

Check out the eco-friendly options listed below and see which ones you do and don't like the look of. Tick the boxes which apply to you for each option.

	Willing to try	Not for me
> Re-useable sanitary towels	◯	◯
> A menstrual cup	◯	◯
> Biodegradable disposable pads	◯	◯
> Period underwear	◯	◯
> Free bleeding (check your wardrobe and see if you have items you don't mind using for this)	◯	◯

Any notes relating to my searches
(e.g., re-useable sanitary towel brands I like the look of)

Fitness

From dance shoes to football boots, boxing gloves to baseballs, it's worth finding out if the sports equipment you're using is made from animals. Although many companies are making huge efforts to move away from using animals in this area, it's still not a guaranteed that everything sports-related is vegan-friendly.

The most common animal products used in sports and fitness equipment are listed below.

Ingredient	What it is	Which products it's often found in
Leather	The skin of a cow or sometimes a pig	Shoes, balls, gloves
Glue	Animal collagen. A process where they will boil animal bones, skins, tendons, and connective tissue.	Shoes
Merino wool	Fibre obtained from the merino sheep	Yoga clothes, active wear, ski boots lining
Fur	The short, fine, soft hair of certain animals, such as racoon, rabbit, fox, and coyote	Ski jackets and hats
Silk	Caterpillar spit (or saliva). Millions of silkworms are boiled, roasted, or frozen alive to cultivate it	Ski suit linings
Cashmere	Fibre obtained from the cashmere goat	Ski hats and clothing

Some brands make it really difficult to know if their items are vegan-friendly, so if you can't easily find the information online, drop them an email to ask outright. Use the below to record what you find out about your favourite brands.

Sports equipment I need/have	If I already have it, is it vegan? If it isn't vegan, what do I need to do?	If I need to buy it, which vegan versions have I found?
e.g., gym trainers	Current trainers need replacing and are not vegan (part leather)	The Vegan 1000 from Pretend Vegan Shoes

CHAPTER FIVE

HOUSEHOLD

Eco living

There are so many opportunities to reduce our impact on animals and the planet in and around the home, sometimes in places we never thought to look before. Eliminating animal products in our homes further reduces suffering.

Furniture and accessories

> When thinking about buying new furniture, consider if you could buy second-hand, or upcycle instead. If you decide to buy new, check that they don't contain any animal products like feathers or leather.

> Even vegan-friendly sofas can come accessorised with feather pillows as standard, which isn't advertised. Double check before ordering.

> Buy sustainably-sourced wood furniture where possible.

> Look out for rugs that may be woven with wool.

> Often, pillows, cushions, and duvets (especially those marketed as 'luxury') will contain feathers.

> Silk is made from the cruel process of boiling cocooned silkworms alive so that their silk can be unravelled, woven, and used for fabric. Silk can be found in soft furnishings around the home (or in fashion).

> If you currently have items that contain animal products, like a leather sofa, you may wish to keep it till the end of its life span to avoid waste, or you may decide to sell it on or donate to charity if you no longer want it in your home.

> Candles can contain beeswax. Shop for soy alternatives and ideally scent-free candles to eliminate toxins.

Kitchen

> If you have the space, invest in a home composting system. Composting our food waste stops it ending up in landfill, avoiding the harmful emissions emitted as landfill breaks down, and is a double win because we end up with lovely, healthy soil to use in our own gardens and plant pots! You can buy compost bins often quite cheaply from your local council or you can create your own out of old wood or pallets. If you don't have a garden, try a space-saving, quick composting method, such as a Bokashi bin, which can live on a worktop or be tucked away in a cupboard.

> Invest in food wraps that are not made from beeswax to help keep packed lunches fresh while on the go.

Garden

> Encourage wildlife by feeding the birds, creating a mini pond for frogs, and building bug boxes or insect hideouts.

> Avoid using chemical insecticides and instead use natural repellents if needed. To deter ants and not harm them, crush raw garlic and place it inside the entrance that the ants are using. You can also make a spray with any or all of the following essential oils: peppermint, lavender, thyme, cedarwood, and star anise. Apply the spray to door thresholds to prevent ants from entering. Repeat daily as needed. Spray also doubles up as a spider repellent. Spray around windows and doors to deter eight-legged friends.

> Help bees and other insects to find food by planting wildflowers.

Have a walk round your house and see what things you own that may have animal products in. Check them off as you go.

Item	Contains animal products	
	Yes	No
> Sofa	○	○
> Cushions	○	○
> Pillows	○	○
> Duvets	○	○
> Rugs	○	○
> Blankets	○	○
>	○	○
>	○	○
>	○	○
>	○	○
>	○	○
>	○	○
>	○	○

Cleaning

Do we really know what's going down our plug hole and where it ends up? Some chemicals in regular cleaners are heavily toxic and are bad for our health, as well as the planet. If you do have heavily chemical-laden products under the sink, try swapping them out for some more natural alternatives. Some cleaning products can even contain animal based ingredients, such as furniture polish which can contain beeswax.

Here are a few examples of good alternative cleaners to start with:

> White vinegar is great at removing stains, disinfecting surfaces, and creating streak-free windows.

> Bicarbonate of soda is a superhero at removing odours, as a mild abrasive, and if mixed with white vinegar, it can help clear blocked plugholes.

> Essential oils are powerhouses when it comes to cleaning. Many have antibacterial properties, such as lemon, tea tree, wild orange, and peppermint, so are great for mixing with water and white vinegar and can be used all over the home.

None of these options contain any of the harmful chemicals that can aggravate our lungs, skin, and eyes. Ideal if you have young children in the house or people with health issues like asthma.

You could also reduce waste when cleaning by ditching disposable wipes that are full of plastic, which take hundreds of years to breakdown, and swapping them for re-useable cloths. You could even use old clothing that is too worn to donate to charity as cleaning rags.

When washing your clothes, some fabric softeners contain animal fat from pigs, cows, sheep, or horses, and like all cleaning products, they may have been tested on animals. If you are buying any shop-bought cleaners, keep an eye out for the Leaping Bunny logo or other certifications to ensure that it is cruelty free and do a quick online search to check the ingredients. Lots of organisations have easily accessible databases showing which brands are and aren't vegan.

Toxic test!

Have a raid of all the cleaning products you use and find out how cruelty-free or planet-friendly they really are. Keep in mind that, if you discover that something you own is not vegan-friendly, you may still want to finish using it to avoid excess waste.

Product	Contains environment damaging ingredients?	Tested on animals?	Notes of potential replacements if needed
Toilet cleaner	Yes – bleach	No	Switch to eco brand. Need to find a cheap one that works.

Product	Contains environment damaging ingredients?	Tested on animals?	Notes of potential replacements if needed

Energy

Saving on energy can help with our carbon footprint and save money in the long run. Here are some ideas for how you can veganise your energy!

> Find an energy supplier that generates their power from renewable, clean sources

> Save on excess energy use around the home where you can

> Turn off lights and anything plugged in when not in use

> Set timers and use a thermostat to control your heating so that you get the best use from it

> Insulate your home as much as possible to improve heat retention

> Save water where possible: you can catch the run-off water while waiting for it to get hot when washing your face or washing up and use it to water the plants or flush the loo.

> Don't wash clothes for the sake of it. If they still smell good, hang them back up and make them last another wear. Washing our clothes too many times damages them, so they'll last longer if you don't over wash them.

> Dry clothes on the line wherever possible to avoid using the tumble dryer. Even if they don't fully dry on the line and you still need to tumble dry them a little when you get them in, they will take less time in the dryer for getting some fresh air into them.

> If you have a woodburning stove or open fire, use seasoned wood that is properly dried, as wet or unseasoned wood contains moisture which, when burned, creates more smoke and harmful particles of air pollution. Alternatively, try using wood briquettes made from compressed dry sawdust and/or wood chips or coffee logs (made from recycled coffee grounds), which burn efficiently and re-uses material that would otherwise have gone to landfill.

CHAPTER SIX

TOOLS FOR SUCCESS

You do you

When you go vegan, some people may think they have the right to challenge you and your decision to go vegan or they might think they know better, whether it be the protein police coming to tell you that you'll perish through lack of nutrition or the wind up merchants that think 'but bacon though' is funny.

Sometimes, choosing to be an ethical vegan can be confusing for others you know if they don't fully understand it. They may feel in some indirect way that you are by default insinuating that they are cruel for not being vegan. There is an interesting study on the hidden biases that drive negative behaviours towards vegans that is well worth a read.[40]

Just remain true to you. Remember why you started down this path in the first place. Learn from others, by all means, but don't be swayed from your truth because of someone else's opinions about what you are doing.

In preparation, you might want to think about the main reasons why you are going vegan. Write them in the spaces on these pages. They are your true north. If you ever feel swayed or belittled or lost, come back to them.

Talking about veganism

When a person goes vegan, naturally, those around them are interested or intrigued and want to find out more or talk about it.

There are two ways to handle these conversations.

1. Politely say you'd rather not discuss it
2. Go all in and discuss or debate

Option 1 – Don't discuss it

It might seem odd to start off a page about conversations by saying that you don't have to have them, but you actually don't have too! You simply might not want to explain yourself or your beliefs or help anyone else understand why you do what you do, or you might just be having a rubbish day and know that you're not in the best place to communicate effectively. That's totally cool. You have complete self-authority to say no.

Option 2 – Have the conversation

The greatest thing to remember if you're feeling a little daunted about the prospect is that you'll usually be walking into the conversation knowing more about veganism than they do as you'll have already been thinking about veganism and researching it and you'll know your reasons for wanting to do it. Don't expect everyone to agree or understand it, just ask for mutual respect and enter into conversations as an equal.

Tell your story
Some vegans find it helpful to tell their story. How you feel about topics such as animal exploitation is valid, and your story and experiences are irrefutable. People can share new information with you that may change your mind on a few things, but ultimately, when you tell people something that is personal to you and your experience, they simply cannot argue with that.

Use facts

Aside from your story, you may also like to centre your approach around facts if that's more your thing (or do both and come at it from all angles!). There are a ton of stats out there proving that ethical veganism is kind to people, animals, and the planet.

Ask questions

Instead of just providing answers or telling people your opinion, you can respond with questions to get the person thinking about how they actually feel about things. Allow them to reach conclusions on their own and highlight flaws or contradictions in their own way of thinking. This approach is very effective in planting seeds and motivating people to change on their terms.

Here are some examples[41]:

Instead of saying: Animal cruelty is wrong
Ask: Do you think animal cruelty is wrong?

Instead of saying: There is no humane way to kill an animal
Ask: Do you think there is a humane way to kill an animal?

Hopefully, your experiences will be friendly and enjoyable, but if there are instances where they aren't or you feel you aren't being listened too, or if you feel offended, you're perfectly within your rights to end the conversation there and walk away.

Use the next couple of pages to keep track of the things you'd like to brush up on or refine for when you talk to people about your vegan lifestyle.

Having conversations about veganism are, in essence, a form of activism. How we approach these conversations is important, and there's some useful information in the 'Activism' chapter of this book that dives more into this area.

If you were on a desert island...

Below are some of the most common things vegans hear. Write in the grid next to them how you'd like to respond.

If you're looking for inspiration on reputable sources of information to help answer these, head to the 'Resources' section for some recommendations.

Common lines vegans hear	How I'd like to respond
Where will you get your protein/calcium from?	
But plants can feel too. They're alive just like animals.	
Humans have always eaten meat, so why should we stop now?	
How could you live without bacon though?	
Animals were put on this earth for us to eat.	
Vegans can't build muscle or be as fit as meat eaters.	

Common lines vegans hear	How I'd like to respond
You'll be deficient in things like iron and B12.	
Humans are carnivores and have canines; we're designed to eat meat.	
If you were on a desert island with no access to a shop, would you kill and eat the animals?	
If the whole world went vegan, we'd be overrun with animals.	
It's okay to kill animals as that's what they were bred for.	
Farming practices in other countries are much worse than they are here.	
How are the dairy and egg industries cruel? Surely I can just be a vegetarian to avoid animal suffering.	

Research

You might be asked questions that you don't know the answers too, which is okay! Researching and thinking about your own viewpoint on issues is key to understanding your place in all of this.

These pages are for you to keep a track of those questions or topics and anything else you want to learn more about.

Look in to:

What I've learned:

Look in to:

What I've learned:

Look in to:

What I've learned:

Look in to:

What I've learned:

Look in to:

What I've learned:

Look in to:

What I've learned:

Look in to:

What I've learned:

Community

Community is important. It helps us learn from others and build up support networks with likeminded people. Sometimes, as a vegan, you might just want to share and discuss food ideas or maybe have a rant about your auntie who wouldn't let up asking you a load of questions at dinner, or maybe you want to learn how you can be more active (more on that in the 'Activism' chapter).

Whatever it is, having people to talk to, who are on the same page as you, can help in so many ways. Try looking for a group that's local to you or an online group that fits with your values. If you are very environmentally focussed, you could join a climate group, or an animal rights group if you want to discuss your ethics with likeminded people.

Two important things you might find helpful when finding your tribe:

1. Know that you will never think exactly the same as another person. Everyone is at a different stage in life, no matter how similar we might be. If you set out to find a group that matches you perfectly, you won't find it. It doesn't exist. Communities are diverse, and it's great when you all want to share wisdom and talk about the same stuff. Be realistic about what you're walking into and expecting from others.

2. The vegan community is a loving and welcoming place, but there are, like any movement, pockets of judgement and perfectionism. Avoid them. If you ever feel you are not being supported to be the best version of you and are instead being berated for what you have or are doing wrong, head for the door. They are not your people! To be clear, this isn't about avoiding people who disagree with you; it can be healthy to have discussions with those whose opinions differ from our own.

Use the template below to keep note of all the groups you might like to become a part of.

Group name:

Location:

Meeting dates/times:

Group name:

Location:

Meeting dates/times:

Group name:

Location:

Meeting dates/times:

Group name:

Location:

Meeting dates/times:

Group name:

Location:

Meeting dates/times:

Group name:

Location:

Meeting dates/times:

My non-vegan life

List all of the non-vegan things in your life. From the things you eat, places you visit, to the clothes you wear. Brainstorm it all so you can get an overview of what you might need to focus on later. This will also help you to think about veganism as a lifestyle choice and realise the parts of your life that veganism affects.

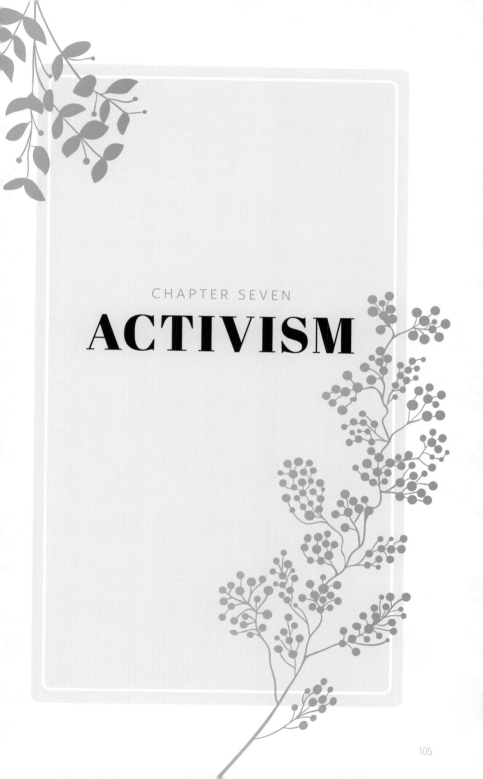

CHAPTER SEVEN

ACTIVISM

Activist

NOUN

A person who campaigns to bring about political or social change.

What activism is all about

It's true that living a vegan life can significantly reduce your impact on the suffering of animals[42] and is the most impactful thing you can do as an individual to reduce your carbon footprint,[43] but vegan activism is about proactive action to promote and encourage change outside of ourselves. It's having a desire to see a more compassionate world where animals are not exploited or killed, where our planet is respected and protected, and where people are aware of how to lead healthy lives without the need for animal products, and it's about taking steps to promote and encourage that.

Activism comes in many forms, and the beauty of it is that we can do what lights us up and makes the best use of our skills and knowledge. We all have different passions, areas we know more about, and importantly, different ways of sharing messages.

In reality, any person who is actively promoting veganism is an activist in their own way, although some are able to commit more time or are more confident to take on bigger projects or more visible roles. But, ultimately, every person makes a difference and is important for the movement.

It's not about making everyone conform to the way you think or feel, it's about sharing information and planting seeds in hearts and minds to help people make their own informed choices.

Even though there are lots more vegan and plant-based options available now, and we've seen many successes in recent times (such as some large fashion designers ditching fur), animal suffering has by no means ended, so it is as important as ever to keep momentum to create global change. The vegan movement is huge, and it needs everybody doing their bit to make it as effective as possible.

The word 'activist' can sometimes be perceived in negative ways, for example, the way we see the media portray some climate activists. In reality, that is far from the truth. Activists are usually people who care deeply and want to make the world a better, not worse, place. It's always advisable to think about your activism and ensure that you are not causing any harm in the process.

So, wherever you are on your activism journey, there is no better time than now to be inspired and get started!

Getting started

Activism comes in many forms. Below are the three main areas to give you an idea of what can be involved.

Systemic change

These are often long-term strategies which involve engaging with politicians or businesses with a large reach. They can include lobbying parliament (a recent success was the banning of selling shark fins in the UK[44]) or engaging with large companies to change their policies, for example, pressuring them to stop selling animal products. You can start these initiatives yourself or you can lend your support to campaigns lead by not-for-profit organisations, charities, or other groups.

Local activism

These are generally grassroots groups. A grassroots movement is one that gathers people in a specific geographical area to target a local issue, e.g., campaigning against the opening of a new factory farm nearby or working with local businesses to expand their vegan offering. You may already have groups operating local to you that are campaigning via street demonstrations or other methods.

Education

This method is broad and wide reaching. It can involve creating and sharing online content or having thought-provoking conversations with people. You could hand out leaflets or you could go into schools or universities and directly educate future generations. Basically, anything that involves planting mental seeds and educating others!

Some other ways vegans might be active:

> Having a membership with an organisation supporting vegan or animal rights causes

> Sharing food and recipes with others

> Attending environmental events, such as beach litter picks

> Volunteering at events, such as fairs, and representing charities or organisations to raise funds or awareness

> Helping at a local animal sanctuary

> Fostering animals in need of love and care whilst they're transitioning to forever homes

> Signing petitions

As you can see, there are LOADS of things you can get involved in!

You might do only one of these, you might do two. You know what? You might do them all in your lifetime! It really doesn't matter how many you do. What matters is that to change the world and make it a better place for all living beings, we must all play our part.

If you'd like to get more active for animals or the planet, use the prompts on the next page to help you discover your strengths, which will guide you to get the best from your activism.

What are my skill sets? What am I good at?
e.g., organisational skills, creating digital content, having meaningful and effective conversations.

Areas I'm interested in becoming active.
e.g., volunteering, educational speaking, creating digital content.

What message do I want the world to hear?

How I plan to get started/build on my current activism.
e.g., making links with my local activist groups, creating a dedicated
YouTube channel for my content.

People will forget
what you said,
people will forget
what you did,
but people will
never forget how
you made them feel.

Maya Angelou

Effective conversations

When advocating for your cause, you want to do it the best you can, so having good, effective conversations is naturally important. Think of every conversation you engage in as having the potential to have a ripple effect outwards, due to the things that person then may change for the better, as well as the conversations they themselves will go on to have as a result.

Here are some golden tips for having effective conversations:

> Accept that people won't always see your point of view. Everyone is on their own journey, but you can plant a seed that may ultimately create change somewhere down the line.

> Go into the conversation with the desire to share knowledge, not to apportion blame or guilt. Show that you are listening too.

> People are rarely willing to change overnight, so encourage them to take steps that work for them. Small steps inevitably lead to bigger steps over time. Celebrate the small wins. Humans respond to praise far better than criticism.

> People may sometimes perceive vegans as thinking they are superior. Find common ground and avoid patronising language. Enter conversations as equals.

> Feeling emotions is a good thing. It is your superpower. Find a balance to make it something that compliments your communication style rather than overpowering it.

> It's okay to say you don't know. You don't have to have all of the answers figured out. This is a continuous learning curve for everyone.

> If you're feeling nervous about lacking expertise, keep in mind that most of the time you will be going into discussions with more knowledge on the topic than the person you're talking too as you've already personally looked into these subjects to understand and apply them in your own life. If in doubt, speak from personal experience.

> People are all at different points in their lives and have whole lifetimes worth of belief systems and values built into them. People also take in information in different ways. Sometimes, your chosen form of activism won't resonate with someone. That's cool. Move on.

There's not a perfect or one right way to do things; just the fact that you've showed up and are trying is the absolute best thing you can be doing!

Knowledge is power!

As an activist, it's handy to know the basics that you might be asked in conversation. You don't need to remember facts and figures if that's not your thing (although it's great if you can or want too!), it's just good to have an overview of the main topics so that you are prepared. Knowledge is power, and you'll feel so much more confident having done some prep work. You can keep a note of the things you research on the dedicated pages in the 'Tools for Success' chapter, or in the notes pages at the back of this journal.

Below are some of the commonly held beliefs and topics that people often want to know more about. The 'Tools for Success' chapter also has some more prompts and tools for topics of conversation.

Animals

> How the dairy and egg industries are cruel
> Why honey is not vegan
> Understanding animals' experience in common factory farming methods
> Knowing what actually happens in a slaughterhouse and what 'humane' slaughter really means
> Understanding animal sentiency and their ability to feel pain

Health

> What foods you can find essential nutrients in (the most common are protein, calcium, iron, and B12)
> How eating a vegan diet can benefit health
> How eating animal products can negatively affect health

Environment

> What impact animal agriculture has on the environment (carbon emissions/waste/water usage)
> How a vegan diet requires less land to produce food compared to a diet containing meat
> The difference between eating meat from local suppliers and globally sourced meat (e.g., meat that comes from a country that is destroying the Amazon rainforest to clear land for cattle grazing)
> Why palm oil may not be vegan

Visualisation and manifestation are powerful techniques.

Think about the world you want to create and dream it into being.

My vision for a better world is ...

Wellbeing

Activist burnout is incredibly common, so it deserves a place in this journal. Being exposed to the global suffering of animals, the injustices of the world, or feeling the impending pressure of the climate emergency can all weigh heavy on activists.

Burnout can look different for everyone, but some of the most common signs are:

> Difficulty sleeping

> Feeling low or depressed

> Overeating or loss of appetite

> Using drugs or alcohol as a means of escape

> Fatigue

> Becoming tearful easily

> Responding to situations with anger where you wouldn't normally

These can be signs of many things, not just burnout, but if you start to feel like you're overwhelmed by the things you are seeing in your activism, it's really important to recognise it and take care of yourself.

Sustainable activism is essential to an effective movement.

It's perfectly okay to have off days and take some time to rest and recuperate. You can't pour from an empty cup, and we advocate much better for our cause when we are emotionally well.

The fact that you are consciously trying to make the world a better place is incredible. The world's problems are not yours to solve alone; you are only one person.

If you do start to feel burnout, here are some things you might like to try doing:

> Talk to people in your support network about how you're feeling, whether they're family and friends or fellow activists

> Ask for support, in whatever form you need it

> Make a list of all the things you have achieved recently or in the past year. Reflecting on achievements is incredibly important as we get to see that, no matter how small we think our actions are, we are making an impact

> Make time to do things you enjoy that don't involve activism

No matter what you do, sometimes burnout is inevitable. You can be as prepared as you like, but it can still arrive at your door, forcing you to face your emotions and take some down time. This is perfectly normal and okay. Feel the feels and take good care of yourself. You deserve it.

What signs do I need to look out for in myself when I start to become burnt-out or run down?

My plan for self-care when I start to feel this way
e.g., getting plenty of sleep, eating healthier, moving your body and getting some exercise, speaking to someone close to you

**Start where you are.
Use what you have.
Do what you can.**

Arthur Ashe

A final note

Hopefully, the sections in this book have equipped you with the tools and knowledge you need to embrace an ethical vegan lifestyle and have empowered you to make changes that are important to you.

Included at the back of this book is a resources section containing the top sources I or others I know have found useful on our vegan journeys, from inspirational speakers to world-leading organisations and actual tools for you to use. It's all there to save you time endlessly searching the internet and get you directly to some golden content.

From the bottom of my heart, thank you for reading this book and incorporating veganism into your life. Animals deserve to live their lives without exploitation or harm for human gain, and we need more compassionate and kind people like you doing their bit all over the planet to create an existence free from animal suffering.

The world is a better place because you care.

Keep being amazing.

Sadie
xo

You are now
part of a cruelty-
free community

Well done, keep
it up, and spread
the word!

Acknowledgements

To Jack, thank you for being in this with me wholeheartedly, every single step of the way. Figuring out life with you is a beautiful adventure. We were written in the stars, and together we are unstoppable.

To my mum, Michelle Wooltorton. Thank you for being the most amazing mum anyone could wish for. We're just a couple of Starseeds here figuring it out, and I hit jackpot when I got you as my guide earth-side. You teach me to stay true to myself and go within, and to always believe in magic. Every new height I reach is because you installed the belief in me that I can do whatever I put my mind too.

To my Dad, Chris Kirk, thank you for believing in me. I've never wanted to make anyone prouder than I do you. You are the best dad a girl could wish for, and I am so blessed to have your unwavering support and encouragement in everything I do. You are my anchor and stability in life, and I'd be lost without you.

To the wise women in my life, Jenny Clarke, Kim Knights, and Dawn Lucht. Thank you for the divine wisdom you've shared with me through the years. You helped me to unlock so many parts within myself and it fundamentally changed my life for the better.

To the small team at Softwood Self-Publishing that helped make this book possible, thank you to every single one of you. Maddy Glenn, my editor and fountain of knowledge for all things publishing, you've been there every step of the way and made this whole thing seamless. Claire Smith, my cover artist, you took my words and turned them into the most beautiful cover design that I just love. Carl Thompson, my designer and formatter, you brought the pages of this book to life transforming it from a caterpillar into a beautiful butterfly. And thank you to my team of beta readers who critiqued this before it went out into the world, your support and feedback meant so much to me: Jack, Leanne, Tina, Kat, Abbie, Jenny, Tommy, Gemma, Andy, Millie, Mum, Amy, and Tash.

To the organisations who supported me in writing this: Animal Aid, The Humane League, and The Vegan Society, thank you for the advice you gave me along the way and for the reviews I will proudly display on the cover of this book.

And finally to my fellow vegans who willingly took part in anonymous surveys and research for this book. Thank you for sharing your stories, your wisdom, and what was important to you in your vegan journeys. You helped shape the foundations of this book.

I am incredibly grateful to be surrounded by so many good humans and animals that bring light and love to my life. There are far too many to write on one page, so to all of you who stand by me and generally do life with me, know that I love you and am thankful for you.

Resources

Below are some great places to start if you're looking for inspiring people or organisations for more vegan-related content. All @ handles relate to Instagram.

Animal Rights and activism

> Animal Aid (www.animalaid.org.uk) – One of the UK's largest animal rights groups. A great hub for campaigns that span all types of animal exploitation

> The Humane League (www.thehumaneleague.org.uk) – Working to end the abuse of animals raised for food by influencing the policies of the world's biggest companies, demanding legislation, and empowering individual action

> Animal Equality UK (www.animalequality.org.uk) – An international organisation working with society, governments, and companies to end cruelty to farmed animals

> Centre for Effective Vegan Advocacy (www.veganadvocacy.org) – Tools to help improve your vegan advocacy

> Surge (www.surgeactivism.org) – Animal rights non-profit spreading awareness, content, campaigns, educational programmes, and investigative work

> Earthling Ed, FREE E-Book: 30 Non-Vegan Excuses & How to Respond to Them (https://earthlinged.org/ebook)

> Viva (www.viva.org.uk) – UK vegan charity campaigning for a kinder, more sustainable world for animals and humans

> PETA (www.peta.org) – Largest animal rights organisation in the world, campaigning for the protection of animals

> Animal Liberation by Peter Singer (book) – An insightful look into ethics and how we treat animals

> Eat Like You Care: An Examination of the Morality of Eating Animals by Gary L Francione and Anna Charlton (book) – Broken down into chapters of common excuses that vegans hear; a great starting point for anyone wanting to know how to respond when having conversations about veganism

- Yuval Noah Harari (search his YouTube videos on animal sentiency) – Philosopher who critically examines human treatments of animals

- Earthling Ed (@earthlinged) – Activist and vegan educator. Ed's videos help you to learn how to debate veganism and understand topics in more detail

- Jake Conroy (@the.cranky.vegan) – Animal rights activist and vegan who critically discusses approaches to activism and general vegan news

- Bite Size Vegan (www.bitesizevegan.org) – Detailed and well-researched educational vegan content

Food

- The Vegan Society (www.vegansociety.com) – Fountain of knowledge for all things vegan-related

- Veganuary (www.veganuary.com) – Support to transition to a vegan lifestyle (free recipes, tips, info, and more)

- BOSH (www.bosh.tv) – Easy to follow vegan recipes

- Mille Barker (@millevegan) – Vegan food inspiration

- Deliciously Ella (www.deliciouslyella.com) – Vegan recipes

- www.barnivore.com – Online directory of vegan alcohol

- Jessica (@love.vegan.soul) – Vegan food inspiration

- www.veganwomble.com – Community blog with more than just food info. A useful source of information for any vegan

- Meghan (@meggythevegan) – Vegan food inspiration

Veganism at work

- The Vegan Network (www.vegannetwork.co.uk) – UK's first Vegan Network in a County Council. Can offer peer support to organisations wanting to start their own vegan initiative in their workplace and are specialists in the public sector

- Vegan Leaders in Corporate Management (www.veganleaders.com) – Provides help to start a vegan initiative in your organisation, alongside peer support and networking with other vegan leaders/professionals

- The Vegan Society (www.vegansociety.com) – Download their 'Employer Workbook: Supporting Vegans in the Workplace'. Ideal if you are an employer or someone wishing to work with their employer to create an inclusive workplace

- Vegan Mainstream (LinkedIn group https://www.linkedin.com/groups/2027865/) – Community of like-minded vegan entrepreneurs and creatives coming together to support each other and build meaningful relationships

Personal care

- Cruelty Free International (www.crueltyfreeinternational.org) – Campaigning to end animal suffering in laboratories. Comprehensive list of cruelty-free suppliers

- PETA (www.peta.org/living/personal-care-fashion/beauty-without-bunnies) – Comprehensive list of brands and companies that do and don't test on animals

- Leaping Bunny (www.leapingbunny.org) – Certification for cruelty-free products

- Cruelty Free Kitty (www.crueltyfreekitty.com) – Experts in cruelty free beauty and personal care

Health and nutrition

- The China Study by T. Colin Campbell and Thomas M. Campbell II (book) – examines the link between the consumption of animal products and chronic illnesses

- The Physicians Committee for Responsible Medicine (www.pcrm.org) – Non-profit changing the way doctors treat and cure diseases using innovative, cruelty-free methods

- The Homegrown Vegan & Holistic Wellbeing (www.thehomegrownvegan.com) – Plant-based nutrition and wellbeing life coaching

- Dr Michael Greger (@nutrition_facts_org) – providing evidence-based nutrition advice

Environmental

> Permacrafters (www.permacrafters.com) – Teaches skills for eco-friendly living

> www.treehugger.com – Offers advice, clarity, and inspiration on all things sustainability

> www.thegoodshoppingguide.com – Compares ethical ratings of the world's leading brands.

Documentaries

> Cowspiracy – Uncovering the real solution to the most pressing environmental issues

> Seaspiracy – Documentary about the environmental impact of fishing

> Dominion – Hidden camera and drone footage investigating the dark side of animal agriculture

> Blackfish – The story of Tilikum, the captive killer whale, and the consequences of keeping orcas in captivity

> Earthlings – Exposing the suffering of animals in factory farms, research labs, puppy mills, and more

> What the Health – Uncovering the secrets to preventing and reversing chronic diseases

> Forks Over Knives – Exploring the possibility that people changing their diets from animal-based to plant-based can help eliminate and control diseases

> Vegucated – Exploring the challenges of converting to a vegan diet

> The Game Changers – Revolutionary film about meat, protein, and strength

Apps

> HappyCow – Find vegan food local to you

> 21-Day vegan kickstart – Make your vegan transition simple with healthy plant-based recipes and nutrition tips developed by expert dieticians and chefs

- **Bunny Free** – Check if products are cruelty-free

- **Is It Vegan?** – Scan items to check if they're vegan

- **Vegan Scan** – Scan barcodes at the supermarket to quickly discover if the item is suitable for vegans

- **Veganalyser** – Calculates how many animals you could save by going vegan

- **Good on you** – Discover ethical brands and see how your favourites measure up

Podcasts

- **The Disclosure Podcast** – Exploring topics surrounding veganism, morality, ethics, communication, and the environment

- **The Simply Vegan Podcast** – Chat, food reviews, recipes, nutrition advice, and interviews

- **The Vegan Gym Podcast** – Evidence-based training and personal development to help get you in the best shape of your life

- **Vegan Abattoir** – Plant-based answers to the vegan curious, taking Q&As from meat eaters and milk drinkers

- **The Plant Based News Podcast** – Pioneering vegan and ethical news

- **Vegan Life Magazine Podcast** – Chat and inspiration for those wanting to adopt a plant-based diet

- **Climate Change for Beginners:** An Extinction Rebellion Podcast – talking climate-based science and answering common Q&As

- **Planet A** – Talks on climate change, talking to world leading experts, policy makers, and activists about climate change and its possible solutions

- **Performing Animal Rights** – Exploring creative practice within the animal rights movement

- **The Vegan Pod** - Hosted by The Vegan Society, discussing a variety of ideas, facts, and opinions on all things vegan

References

[1] G. Hussain (2021, December. 17). How Many Animals Are Killed for Food Every Day? [Online]. Available: https://sentientmedia.org/how-many-animals-are-killed-for-food-every-day

[2] ASPCA (2015). A Growing Problem. Selective Breeding in the Chicken Industry: The Case for Slower growth. [Online PDF]. Available: https://www.aspca.org/sites/default/files/chix_white_paper_nov2015_lores.pdf

[3] Z. O'Brien (2018, August. 4). 'Bringing home the bacon has never been crueller': Shoppers buying 'high welfare' pork have been 'misled' for 15 years after Government failed to act on its own advice on co2 slaughters [Online]. Available: www.dailymail.co.uk/news/article-6016465/Pigs-die-kicking-screaming-packaged-high-welfare-meat-products.html

[4] BBC (2020, January. 7). Confessions of a slaughterhouse worker [Online]. Available: www.bbc.co.uk/news/stories-50986683

[5] F. Harvey (2021, May. 12). Animals to be formally recognised as sentient beings in UK law [Online]. Available: www.theguardian.com/world/2021/may/12/animals-to-be-formally-recognised-as-sentient-beings-in-uk-law

[6] M. Springman, H.C.J. Godfray, M. Rayner, P. Scarborough (2016, February. 9). Analysis and valuation of the health and climate change cobenefits of dietary change [Online PDF]. Available: www.pnas.org/content/pnas/113/15/4146.full.pdf

[7] Physicians Committee for Responsible Medicine (2019, April. 8). Vegan Diets Reduce the Risk for Chronic Disease [Online]. Available: https://www.pcrm.org/news/health-nutrition/vegan-diets-reduce-risk-chronic-disease

[8] T.C. Campbell, T.M. Campbell II, The China Study, 2nd ed. Texas: Dallas, BenBella Books, 2016

[9] C. Sudlow (2019, January. 3). Should you give up meat for good? [Online]. Available: www.bhf.org.uk/what-we-do/news-from-the-bhf/news-archive/2019/january/the-best-sustainable-diet

[10] Life Bistro (n.d.). How Veganism Can Improve Your Mental Health [Online]. Available: www.lifebistroatl.com/lifestyle/how-veganism-can-improve-your-mental-health

[11] T. Levitt (2020, September. 15). Covid and farm animals: nine pandemics that changed the world [Online]. Available: www.theguardian.com/environment/ng-interactive/2020/sep/15/covid-farm-animals-and-pandemics-diseases-that-changed-the-world

[12] J. Dalton (2021, January. 30). Meat-eating creates risk of future pandemic that 'would make Covid seem a dress rehearsal', scientists warn [Online]. Available: www.independent.co.uk/climate-change/news/meat-coronavirus-pandemic-science-animals-b1794996.html

[13] M. Springmann, M. Clark, D. Mason-D'Cros, et al., "Options for keeping the food system within environmental limits", Nature, vol. 562, pp. 519–525, Oct 2018. Available: https://doi.org/10.1038/s41586-018-0594-0

[14] Food and Agriculture Organization of the United Nations (2013). Tackling Climate Change Through Livestock [Online PDF]. Available: https://www.fao.org/3/i3437e/i3437e.pdf

[15] K. Block (2021, October. 14). Here's why animal agriculture must be central at UN climate

change summit [Online]. Available: https://blog.humanesociety.org/2021/10/animal-agriculture-must-be-central-un-climate-change-summit.html

[16] O. Petter (2020, September. 24). Veganism is 'Single Biggest Way' to Reduce Our Environmental Impact, Study Finds [Online]. Available: https://www.independent.co.uk/life-style/health-and-families/veganism-environmental-impact-planet-reduced-plant-based-diet-humans-study-a8378631.html

[17] F. Harvey (2021, March. 31). Destruction of world's forests increased sharply in 2020 [Online]. Available: www.theguardian.com/environment/2021/mar/31/destruction-of-worlds-forests-increased-sharply-in-2020-loss-tree-cover-tropical

[18] WWF (2020). The Hidden costs of burgers [Online]. Available: https://wwf.panda.org/discover/knowledge_hub/where_we_work/amazon/amazon_threats/unsustainable_cattle_ranching/#:~:text=Habitat%20conversion%2C%20commonly%20referred%20to,2008).

[19] D. Carrington (2018, March. 12). What is biodiversity and why does it matter to us? [Online]. Available: https://www.theguardian.com/news/2018/mar/12/what-is-biodiversity-and-why-does-it-matter-to-us

[20] H. Ritchie (2021, March. 4). If the world adopted a plant-based diet we would reduce global agricultural land use from 4 to 1 billion hectares [Online]. Available: https://ourworldindata.org/land-use-diets

[21] J. Robbins, Diet for a New America: How Your Choices Affect Your Health, Happiness & the Future of Life on Earth, US, New Hampshire: Walpole, H J Kramer, 1998

[22] O. Milman (2017, August. 1). Meat industry blamed for largest-ever 'dead zone' in Gulf of Mexico [Online]. Available: https://www.theguardian.com/environment/2017/aug/01/meat-industry-dead-zone-gulf-of-mexico-environment-pollution

[23] Biological Diversity (n.d.). Take extinction off your plate [Online]. Available: https://www.biologicaldiversity.org/takeextinctionoffyourplate/extinction_facts/pdfs/BurgerFactsheet.pdf

[24] Sea Shepherd (2019, August. 22). The Most Dangerous Single Source of Ocean Plastic No One Wants to Talk About [Online]. Available: https://www.seashepherdglobal.org/latest-news/marine-debris-plastic-fishing-gear/

[25] A. Simke (2020). There Is Plastic In Your Fish [Online]. Available: https://www.forbes.com/sites/ariellasimke/2020/01/21/there-is-plastic-in-your-fish/?sh=4c69ca7b7071

[26] T. Riley (2017). Just 100 companies responsible for 71% of global emissions, study says [Online]. Available: https://www.theguardian.com/sustainable-business/2017/jul/10/100-fossil-fuel-companies-investors-responsible-71-global-emissions-cdp-study-climate-change

[27] BBC (2020, January. 3). Ethical veganism is philosophical belief, tribunal rules [Online]. Available: https://www.bbc.co.uk/news/uk-50981359

[28] The Vegan Society (2022). What rights do vegans have? [Online]. Available: https://www.vegansociety.com/get-involved/international-rights-network/what-rights-do-vegans-have

[29] L. Bandoim (2020). The Shocking Amount Of Food US Households Waste Every Year [Online]. Available: www.forbes.com/sites/lanabandoim/2020/01/26/the-shocking-amount-of-food-us-households-waste-every-year/

[30] Food and Agriculture Organization of the United Nations (2022). International Day of Awareness of Food Loss and Waste [Online]. Available: https://www.fao.org/international-day-awareness-food-loss-waste

[31] H. Constable (n.d.). Your brand new returns end up in landfill [Online]. Available: www.bbcearth.com/news/your-brand-new-returns-end-up-in-landfill

[32] A. Knight and Ma. Leitsberger, "Vegetarian versus Meat-Based Diets for Companion Animals", Animals, vol. 6, no. 9, p. 57, Sep. 2016, doi: 10.3390/ani6090057.

[33] J. Webber (2021, August. 26). Could A Vegan Diet Actually Be Better For Dogs Than Meat? [Online] Available: https://plantbasednews.org/opinion/vegan-dogs/

[34] Animal Aid (n.d.). Animal Experiments: Killing Animals and Humans [Online]. Available: https://www.animalaid.org.uk/the-issues/our-campaigns/animal-experiments/killing-animals-humans/

[35] Queensland Health (2020, November). Medicines/pharmaceuticals of animal origin [Online PDF]. Available: https://www.health.qld.gov.au/__data/assets/pdf_file/0024/147507/qh-gdl-954.pdf

[36] Gov.uk (2021, January. 15). Guide to the use of human and animal products in vaccines [Online]. Available: https://www.gov.uk/government/publications/use-of-human-and-animal-products-in-vaccines/guide-to-the-use-of-human-and-animal-products-in-vaccines

[37] E.M. Barwick (2021, July. 14). Are Tampons Vegan? Are They SAFE? [Online] Available: bitesizevegan.org/ethics/are-tampons-vegan-are-they-safe

[38] A. Laughlin (2021, June. 28). The Ultimate Guide to Having a Cruelty-Free Period [Online]. Available: www.crueltyfreekitty.com/bath-body/cruelty-free-feminine-hygiene

[39] L. Rodriguez (2021, May. 27). Which Period Products are Best for the Environment? [Online] Available: www.globalcitizen.org/en/content/best-period-products-for-the-environment

[40] Z. Gorvett (2020, February. 2020) The hidden biases that drive anti-vegan hatred [Online]. Available: https://www.bbc.com/future/article/20200203-the-hidden-biases-that-drive-anti-vegan-hatred

[41] Earthling Ed, An E-Book for Vegans: 30 Non-Vegan Excuses & How to Respond to Them. UK: Earthling Ed, 2021 [Online]. Available: https://drive.google.com/file/d/1aeM4QiOUE3pP134QlgGlOh5vnQs9vdzY/view

[42] Animal Aid (2022). Going vegan for the animals [Online]. Available: https://www.animalaid.org.uk/veganism/why-veganism/going-vegan-animals/

[43] J. Poore, T. Nemecek, "Reducing food's environmental impacts through producers and consumers", Science, vol. 360, issue 6392, pp. 987-992., June 2018.

[44] E. Baker (2021, September. 7). 'Indescribably Cruel' Shark Fin Trade To Be Banned In UK, Government Confirms [Online]. Available: https://plantbasednews.org/culture/law-and-politics/shark-fin-trade-banned-uk

Notes

Notes

Notes

Notes

About the Author

Sadie is a passionate animal rights activist and speaker who is widely known for empowering others to advocate for animals and the planet. She regularly delivers talks on ethical veganism and animal rights topics, both virtually and in person at schools, universities, and groups all over the country. Sadie is co-founder of The Vegan Network, which provides a platform and voice to vegans in local government. She is a freelance writer, with guest publications and blogs for organisations including Veganuary and Vegan Life Magazine.

You can find her at www.sadiejade.com